THE HISTORY OF NATIONS

Afghanistan

THE HISTORY OF NATIONS

Afghanistan

Other books in the History of Nations series:

The History of Nations

Afghanistan

Thomas Streissguth, *Book Editor*

Bruce Glassman, *Vice President*
Bonnie Szumski, *Publisher*
Helen Cothran, *Managing Editor*

GREENHAVEN PRESS
An imprint of Thomson Gale, a part of The Thomson Corporation

958.1
AFG

Detroit • New York • San Francisco • San Diego • New Haven, Conn.
Waterville, Maine • London • Munich

For more information, contact
Greenhaven Press
27500 Drake Rd.
Farmington Hills, MI 48331-3535
Or you can visit our Internet site at http://www.gale.com

Cover credit: © Bridgeman. This giant standing Buddha built in Afghanistan's Bamian Valley in the fifth or sixth century was destroyed by the Taliban regime in 2001.

LIBRARY OF CONGRESS CATALOGING-IN-PUBLICATION DATA
Afghanistan / Thomas Streissguth, book editor.
p. cm. — (History of nations)
Includes bibliographical references and index.
ISBN 0-7377-1862-5 (lib. bdg. : alk. paper)
1. Afghanistan—History. I. Streissguth, Thomas, 1958– . II. History of nations (Greenhaven Press)
DS356.A325 2006
958.1—dc22   2005045286

Contents

attempt to escape the country, the Communist leader became a prisoner in Kabul.

Chapter 4: The Taliban Era

Chapter 5: The Current Challenges

and remains a potent threat to the government in
Kabul.

FOREWORD

I n 1841, the journalist Charles MacKay remarked, "In read-
ing the history of nations, we find that, like individuals, they
have their whims and peculiarities, their seasons of excitement and recklessness." At the time of MacKay's observation,
many of the nations explored in the Greenhaven Press History
of Nations series did not yet exist in their current form. Nonetheless, whether it is old or young, every nation is similar to an
individual, with its own distinct characteristics and unique story.

The History of Nations series is dedicated to exploring these
stories. Each anthology traces the development of one of the
world's nations from its earliest days, when it was perhaps no
more than a promise on a piece of paper or an idea in the mind
of some revolutionary, through to its status in the world today.
Topics discussed include the pivotal political events and power
struggles that shaped the country as well as important social and
cultural movements. Often, certain dramatic themes and events
recur, such as the rise and fall of empires, the flowering and decay of cultures, or the heroism and treachery of leaders. As well,
in the history of most countries war, oppression, revolution, and
deep social change feature prominently. Nonetheless, the details
of such events vary greatly, as does their impact on the nation
concerned. For example, England's "Glorious Revolution" of
1688 was a peaceful transfer of power that set the stage for the
emergence of democratic institutions in that nation. On the
other hand, in China, the overthrow of dynastic rule in 1912 led
to years of chaos, civil war, and the eventual emergence of a
Communist regime that used violence as a tool to root out opposition and quell popular protest. Readers of the Greenhaven
Press History of Nations series will learn about the common
challenges nations face and the different paths they take in response to such crises. However a nation's story may have developed, the series strives to present a clear and unbiased view of the
country at hand.

The structure of each volume in the series is designed to help
students deepen their understanding of the events, movements,

and persons that define nations. First, a thematic introduction provides critical background material and helps orient the reader. The chapters themselves are designed to provide an accessible and engaging approach to the study of the history of that nation involved and are arranged either thematically or chronologically, as appropriate. The selections include both primary documents, which convey something of the flavor of the time and place concerned, and secondary material, which includes the wisdom of hindsight and scholarship. Finally, each book closes with a detailed chronology, a comprehensive bibliography of suggestions for further research, and a thorough index.

The countries explored within the series are as old as China and as young as Canada, as distinct in character as Spain and India, as large as Russia, and as compact as Japan. Some are based on ethnic nationalism, the belief in an ethnic group as a distinct people sharing a common destiny, whereas others emphasize civic nationalism, in which what defines citizenship is not ethnicity but commitment to a shared constitution and its values. As human societies become increasingly globalized, knowledge of other nations and of the diversity of their cultures, characteristics, and histories becomes ever more important. This series responds to the challenge by furnishing students with a solid and engaging introduction to the history of the world's nations.

INTRODUCTION

L andlocked, remote, divided, and poor, twenty-first-century Afghanistan seems an unlikely place for the world's close attention. However, Afghanistan has been a feature of newspaper headlines for many years. In the 1980s Afghan guerrillas successfully resisted an invasion by the Soviet Union, a military superpower. In the 1990s the Afghans were subject to a strict Islamic government, known as the Taliban, which served as a model for fundamentalist Muslims from Morocco to Indonesia. The Taliban government also harbored al Qaeda, the Islamic terrorist organization responsible for the September 11, 2001, terrorist attacks on the United States. In late 2001 a coalition led by the United States attacked Afghanistan, conquered the capital of Kabul, and overthrew the Taliban government. Afghanistan then began a long and difficult transition to a more secular government, which is still struggling to overcome the country's divisions.

Social conditions within Afghanistan have played an important role in these events. Afghanistan is divided into several isolated regions, which are dominated by ethnic groups separated by different languages, religious beliefs, culture, and history. These groups pay more allegiance to their own leaders than to the Afghan government. Within each ethnic group, clans and tribes fight over land, trade, water, and political authority. As a result, a sense of nationhood and common purpose has eluded the Afghans throughout their history. Overcoming the centuries-old ethnic divisions of Afghanistan is the key task of any Afghan government, a task essential for ending the civil strife and war that has plagued the country for many decades.

Ethnic Groups in Afghanistan

Researchers have identified more than fifty ethnic groups and subgroups in Afghanistan. The dominant ethnic group, the Sunni Muslim Pashtuns, make up about 38 percent of the total population. Hazaras, who are Shiite Muslims, account for another 20 percent of the population and live in the central, mountainous region of the country. Tajiks, who are mostly Sunni Muslims and who speak Persian, comprise approximately 25 percent of the Afghan population. The Uzbeks and Turkomen are Sunni Muslims who speak Turkic dialects and make up another 12 percent of the population. The remaining 5 percent of the population consists of various smaller ethnic groups, including the Baluchis, Aimak, Kyrgyz, and Nuristanis.

Most Afghan kings and prime ministers have been Pashtun, and this group has long controlled the government. Because the Pashtuns have historically been the most powerful ethnic group, the outside world has considered them as representative of all Afghans. As scholar Carol J. Riphenburg explains, "Pashtuns controlled political power for most of Afghanistan's history as a state, with the result that their traditions and cultural precepts tended to be equated with the national identity of Afghanistan."[1]

The Soviet invasion of the 1980s and the civil war that followed disrupted the Pashtun leadership of Afghanistan, allowing smaller ethnic groups to contest Pashtun dominance. The strongest of these were the Tajiks, who make up a relatively well-educated and prosperous class of merchants, farmers, and city dwellers. During the mid-1990s the leader of the Tajik Jamiat-i-Islami Party, Burhanuddin Rabbani, became the president of Afghanistan. However, the resistance of the Pashtuns to Tajik leadership allowed the Taliban, most of whom were Pashtun, to undermine the Afghan government and win control of the country in 1996.

The Taliban instituted a repressive and brutal regime based on the fundamentalist interpretation of Islam preached by their leaders. They carried out massacres of ethnic Hazaras, whom they saw as Shiite infidels, and fought continuously against the Tajiks of the Panjshir Valley in the north, a zone that resisted Taliban control throughout their regime. The Taliban were also opposed by the Uzbeks in the north, who played an important role in defeating them during the U.S.-led campaign in the fall of 2001.

After the fall of the Taliban, central authority disappeared in Afghanistan, which again splintered into a patchwork of semi-independent fiefdoms. The war had strengthened the Afghan warlords, who were used as proxies by the anti-Taliban coalition. These strongmen ruled certain cities and regions with private militias and traded in arms and contraband such as opium. In an article in the *Nation*, journalist Christian Parenti describes the new Afghanistan as "an embryonic narco-mafia state, where politics rely on paramilitary networks engaged in everything from poppy farming, heroin processing, and vote rigging to extortion and the commercial smuggling of commodities like electronics and auto parts."[2]

The warlords controlled tax collection, the justice system, police, schools, and other public institutions. They manipulated traditional village councils known as *shuras*. They also dispensed favors to local families and determined who would represent their region in the capital. The warlords used the threat of violence to extort money from businesses, farmers, and travelers. Any new Afghan president would have to find a way to win some acceptance among the warlords, who had no personal interest in improving Afghanistan's social ills.

A New Start: The Bonn Agreement

The Bonn Agreement, signed by several Afghan leaders in December 2001, outlined a new plan for a representative government in Afghanistan and set up a provisional administration for six months. In June 2002 Afghan tribal leaders met in a *loya jirga*, or grand council, to decide on a provisional prime minister and name a temporary government, known as the Interim Authority.

The *loya jirga* had to create a balance of power among Afghanistan's strongest ethnic groups. The council appointed members of Shura-i Nazar-i Shamali, or Supervisory Council of the North, dominated by ethnic Tajiks, to most of the important posts. A Pashtun tribal leader, Hami Karzai, was appointed temporary president. Karzai eventually won the presidential election of 2004 with 55 percent of the vote. He won a majority of votes in the capital of Kabul, but lost in the outlying regions, where voters showed more loyalty to their ethnic kin and to the warlords who ruled them.

Once in office, Karzai faced a daunting task. The Taliban regime had left Afghanistan without a functioning government. The country had no legislature, no courts, no army, and no civil service. The Taliban had closed down the schools and kept every Afghan female out of work and public life. Afghanistan also had no working hospitals and no health service, and doctors and engineers had fled the country. Fighting and banditry were common in the countryside, and dangerous minefields left over from many years of war were killing and maiming Afghan civilians, especially children.

After his inauguration Karzai took steps to bring Afghanistan's minority ethnic groups into his government. He also followed two important requirements set down by the constitution: All ministers were required to have a college degree, and all had to give up their foreign citizenship and foreign passports. The writers of the constitution wanted educated officials whose first loyalty would be to Afghanistan. They also believed that well-educated officials would be more likely to understand the importance of creating a centralized representative government in Afghanistan rather than trying to build power for their own ethnic groups.

On December 23, 2004, the new president named his cabinet of ministers. He appointed a Pashtun, Abdul Rahim Wardak, as defense minister, replacing the Tajik warlord Muhammed Fahim Mohammad. Ismail Khan, a warlord of Tajik origin and the governor of Herat Province, was named minister of energy and water. Khan was one of the most powerful warlords in Afghanistan, and Karzai's appointment was meant to bring this potential rival to the capital and keep him under control. In a further attempt to strengthen his government and co-opt the warlords, Karzai commissioned some as officers in the national army.

In the first speeches to his country and to the international community, Karzai promised a new era of peace and unity. However, for many Afghans, he remains only the president of Kabul, and his government's authority does not extend into the countryside. Thousands of foreign troops in and around the capital secure the new government, as does the flow of aid from the United States and Western Europe. However, troops and money in Kabul are not enough to force the allegiance of tribal and ethnic leaders who hold power in local governments.

Afghanistan's Uncertain Future

Despite the new government's efforts, tribal leaders in Afghanistan still struggle to keep control of their own regions, which is not surprising given the country's geography and history. Afghanistan is a ruggedly mountainous country with poor roads and communications. These conditions isolate people living in rural provinces, who know they must depend on local chiefs for services and for the protection of their homes and families. In addition, many years of civil war have fractured Afghan society. In their March 2004 report *Establishing the Rule of Law in Afghanistan*, authors Laurel Miller and Robert Perito state that "in most

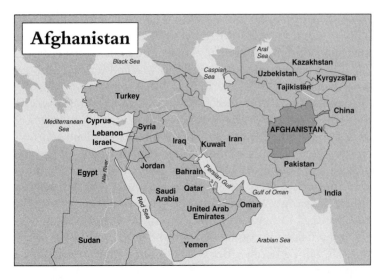

of Afghanistan, the rule of law has never been strong, but after 23 years of warfare, it has been displaced almost completely by the 'rule of the gun.'... The discontinuity of regimes ... has left a patchwork of differing and overlapping laws."[3]

Afghanistan also faces the challenge of eradicating the opium trade that has wildly expanded since the fall of the Taliban. According to one estimate, this trade brings in five times as much money as the national budget of Afghanistan. Opium farmers turn the harvest over to warlords or pay a heavy tax on the money they make by selling their crop. In a 2003 speech introducing a UN report on the opium trade, Antonio Maria Costa, director of the United Nations Office on Drugs and Crime, reported that "the country is clearly at a crossroads; either major surgical drug control measures are taken now, or the drug cancer in Afghanistan will keep spreading and metastasize into corruption, violence and terrorism."[4]

In 2005 Afghanistan began its participation in Plan Afghanistan, a program created by the United States to curtail the opium trade. The United States has budgeted $780 million to reduce Afghan opium production and smuggling. Under the plan, Afghan opium farmers will be paid to grow other crops and find alternative livelihoods. The United States will also attempt to eradicate the poppy fields that supply the opium by engaging in aerial spraying. As of this writing, Plan Afghanistan has only begun to be implemented. Some commentators believe that if the plan fails and opium cultivation continues, the chances for Afghan unity are slim. Journalist Matthew Quirk predicts that "Afghanistan will continue as a failed state run by militias, drug cartels, rebels, and terrorist groups, all well financed and warring over the drug trade."[5]

Avoiding such a future depends on weakening the power of the warlords and disbanding and disarming their private armies. In addition, some experts argue that international aid and foreign investments are vital if Afghanistan is to achieve economic growth and stability. If it does not get such help, the country may continue to suffer from the poverty that exacerbates the ethnic divisions. According to the *Economist*, the nations that have pledged to help Afghanistan must be accountable. If Afghanistan fails to become a successful democracy, the *Economist* says, "It will be because the world's richest countries failed to keep their promises."[6]

Notes

1. Carol J. Riphenburg, "Ethnicity and Civil Society in Contemporary Afghanistan," *Middle East Journal*, vol. 59, no. 1, Winter 2005, p. 31.

2. Christian Parenti, "Who Rules Afghanistan?" *Nation*, November 15, 2004, p. 13.

3. Laurel Miller and Robert Perito, *Special Report: Establishing the Rule of Law in Afghanistan*. Washington, DC: United States Institute of Peace, March 2004, p. 1.

4. Quoted in United Nations Information Service, "Area Under Opium Poppy Cultivation in Afghanistan Has Increased by Eight Percent, UN Says," October 29, 2003. www.unodc.org/unodc/press_release_2003-10-29_1.html.

5. Matthew Quirk, "The New Opium War: A U.S.-Backed Anti-Drug Initiative May Be the Only Way to Keep Afghanistan from Falling Apart," *Atlantic Monthly*, March 2005, p. 52.

6. *Economist*, "Dreams and Promises: Afghanistan's Election," October 16, 2004, p. 14.

The History of Nations

Chapter 1

Early History

Afghanistan's Ethnic Patchwork

By Arnold Fletcher

Many ethnic groups with distinct customs, beliefs, and appearances make up the nation of Afghanistan. Understanding the history and culture of these groups is essential to understanding the rivalries that threaten the country's fledgling democracy in the twenty-first century. In this excerpt from his book Afghanistan: Highway of Conquest, *historian Arnold Fletcher describes Afghanistan's major ethnic groups, including the Pashtuns (or Pushtoons), who have long dominated Afghan society. He notes that scholars disagree about the origins of the Pashtuns. According to their own tradition, the group originated in Palestine and migrated to western Afghanistan during biblical times. However, some ethnologists trace Pashtun origins to an ancient tribe in the Hindu Kush Mountains bordering modern-day Afghanistan and Pakistan. Fletcher also discusses the history and culture of the Tajiks, the Uzbeks, and the Turkomen. In addition, he highlights the important role of religion, tribalism, and the code of Pashtun law in Afghan society.*

Afghanistan is largely an ethnic mystery. The geography that has made it a corridor of travel in Asia has also brought to it a series of visitors—Indo-Aryans, Sakas, Parthians, Persians, Kushans, Greeks, Mongols, Huns, Turks, and others whose names have vanished from legend. Many of these were transients; others halted among the Afghan hills, where the long process of blending and adaptation, in the absence of written record, makes tracing their ethnogenesis almost impossible.

In recent years scholars have begun to examine the Afghan ethnic groups; but anthropometric and serological evidence is still scanty, and historic sources are fragmentary and inconclusive. Thus the question of Afghan origins has evoked more controversy than consensus.

Nevertheless, any attempt to understand their history demands some knowledge of the varied peoples who comprise the Afghan nation. Loyalties and rivalries among these groups are fundamental to the Afghan past, and remain a problem in the present. . . .

Afghan and Pushtoon Origins

Although every citizen of Afghanistan is an Afghan, in a historic sense the name belongs to the people known as Pushtoons, Pukhtoons, or Pathans. These latter speak a language called Pushto or Pukhto, of the Iranian branch of the Indo-European linguistic family and thus related to Persian, Baluchi, and Kurdish, although not derived from any of them. Pushto and Pukhto are dialects of the same language, differing chiefly in that a letter pronounced as a sibilant in Pushto becomes a guttural in Pukhto. Some linguistic authorities maintain that Pushto was the original form and Pukhto a later development; accordingly, for the sake of clarity and since the Durranis, the dominant tribe in Afghanistan from its inception, are Pushto-speakers, the words *Pushto* and *Pushtoon* will be used throughout, even in the occasional references to the "hard" dialect and those who speak it.

The origin and meaning of *Afghan*, once a synonym for Pushtoon, are unknown. One of its first recorded appearances is the *Hudud-al-Alam* ("Regions of the World"), a work of uncertain authorship which appeared around A.D. 980 and contained a tantalizing reference to "Saul, a pleasant village on a mountain. In it live Afghans." The name occurs again in the writings of Mohammed ibn-Ahmad al-Biruni (circa A.D. 1060), who comments, "In the western frontier mountains of India live various tribes of Afghans."

The casualness of these remarks is the more surprising since the Afghans (Pushtoons) make up almost half the population of Afghanistan and have dominated the nation since its beginning. Moreover, al-Biruni lived and wrote at the court of Sultan Mahmud Ghaznawi, whose armies were largely composed of Pushtoons. Most probably the name *Afghan* was originally applied to only a few of the Pushto tribes and later adopted by all of them. This development must have been fairly recent, for as late as A.D. 1809 the name Afghan was "known to the Afghauns themselves only through the medium of the Persian language. Their own name for their nation is Pushtoon, in the plural, Pushtooneh."

The name *Pushtoon* appears to have greater antiquity, even though its rarity in the writings of the past is likewise remarkable. [The ancient Greek historian] Herodotus on a number of occasions mentions the Paktuike or Paktues, whom he describes as serving [Persian king] Xerxes in Greece, wearing skins and carrying the bow. Some authorities consider these people to have been Pushtoons; others are less certain. The incompleteness of Pushtoon ethnography applies equally to many other Afghan ethnic groups.

According to their own tradition, the Pushtoons originated in Palestine in the days of King Saul from whom they claim descent through a son Irmia (Jeremiah), and a grandson, Afghana. They maintain that they grew great in Israel, where they were favorites of David and Solomon, and where the latter assigned them to guard the temple from the assaults of jealous demons. To aid them in this task, Solomon, master of the djinns and afreets, taught the Afghans Pushto, the language of hell. The statement is confirmed by the Prophet Mohammed, according to Afghan tradition, and may be said to acquire some faint credence from the nature of the language itself.

At this time there appeared a wicked magician, Bukht ud-Nasir (Nebuchadnezzar), who scattered the tribes of Israel and sent the Afghans, as the most obstreperous, far to the east, to the lands of Sham or Syria. From here they migrated to the mountains of Ghor in western Afghanistan, where they settled, adhering to the one God although surrounded by countless idolaters. In the time of the Prophet Mohammed, the legend continues, a chief of the Afghans, Qais or Kish, visited Mecca and embraced Islam, receiving the new name of Abdul Rashid. He returned to Afghanistan to convert his people; and from him, through his sons Sarban and Ghurghusht, and a daughter, Bibi Matto, all the present Pushtoons are descended.

This romantic genealogy aroused much interest in Victorian England at a time when the fate of the Ten Lost Tribes ranked as a public issue hardly less burning than the Balkan question. Modern scholars, however, point out that Pushto is an Indo-European rather than a Semitic language, and that its Semitic words are Arabic accretions. There is no mention of Afghana or the Afghans in either Hebrew or Arabic records until long after the time of Mohammed; when they do appear in the latter, the Afghans are usually called Suleimani, an indication that their homeland was in the Suleiman Range [of modern central Pakistan] rather than in the western mountains of Ghor. Also, it has been a common practice in Moslem lands to invent genealogies connecting their people to Mohammed or the other prophets of Islam.

There is still no complete agreement on Pushtoon origins. Afghan scholars often trace them to the people of ancient Bactria,[1] but a number of non-Afghan authorities believe the Pushtoons arrived from the north at a later date. Quite probably they were once a small group centered in the Suleiman Mountains, who were later joined by migrants who adopted their language and customs. There is some evidence in the writings of Arab geographers that the Ghilzai, today one of the larger Pushtoon tribes, are at least in part descended from the Khalaj or Khallukk, a people of Oghuz Turk or Epthalite Hun background.

Modern Pushtoon Society

Although no census has been taken, the Pushtoons are estimated to number about six million in Afghanistan, or about half its population, plus about five million living east of the Afghan border. They have been the dominant people in Afghanistan since its beginning as a nation and the country is, in fact, a Pushtoon creation. Within Afghanistan they are largely concentrated in the east and south, although in recent years a number have been settled north of the Hindu Kush. Regardless of their dispersal, Pushtoons exhibit strong similarities both of custom and of ethnic personality. The tribes, subtribes, and clans into which they are divided are invariably agnates [related through the male side] and usually bear the name of an eponymous ancestor with the addition of *i* ("of") *zai* ("sons of") *khel* ("band of") as, for example, in *Waziri, Mohammedzai,* or *Suleiman Khel.* Loyalty to the tribe or clan varies from group to group but is usually strong; at the same time all Pushtoons have an extreme pride in their Pushtoon identity.

Pushtoons in the past have shown little interest in trade, industry, or urban living. Today they are mostly sedentary agriculturists; but about one million are nomads, moving over considerable distances with their black tents, their camels, and their flocks of sheep. These *Kuchis* [nomads] carry on extensive commerce with the settled folk through whose lands they pass, exchanging animal products for grain, and they are also a problem for the non-

1. a region lying between the Hindu Kush Mountains and the Amu Darya River

Pushtoons because their tempers are uncertain and they often go formidably armed. A number are camel merchants who bring their wares to otherwise inaccessible parts of the country.

Settled Pushtoons are rarely sharecroppers or tenant farmers of the type common in the Middle East. They are most commonly freeholders, but a number are landlords, employing non-Pushtoons as tenants or laborers—a status that may have contributed to the independence and sense of personal worth and dignity that are typical of the Pushtoon personality.

The Pushtoon Style

Since their first recorded appearance, the Pushtoons have been characterized as turbulent, warlike, predatory, and revengeful. [Arab traveler] Ibn Batuta, who met them in A.D. 1333, said they were "mostly highwaymen"; Timur-i-Leng [Tamerlane], a century later, concurred—praise from Caesar indeed. The Pushtoon poet Khushal Khan-i-Khattak described his people as "malevolent, ruthless, and contentious." [German scholar] Adam Olearius in the seventeenth century began a string of the usual unfavorable European comments by calling them a "self-conceited, insolent, cruel, and barbarous people. They slight others for no other reason than that they are not so rash as themselves in hazarding their lives without any necessity."

Statements like this could be multiplied, particularly those from the memoirs of British soldiers and officials of the nineteenth century. They contain, however, only a shred of the truth. Pushtoons have undoubtedly been aggressive, belligerent, and prone to feud and faction—traits that might logically be expected in the circumstances. Since the Pushtoons have always reacted violently to foreign pressure or any threat to their freedom, the reports of invaders could likewise hardly be expected to show much objectivity.

A different point of view was expressed by Mountstuart Elphinstone, who in 1809 headed the first official British mission to Afghanistan. A scholar and linguist, Elphinstone gave a description of the Afghan character that remains sound to the present day. He found them "fond of liberty, faithful to their friends, kind to their dependents, hospitable, brave, hardy, frugal, laborious, and prudent; and they are less disposed than the nations in their neighborhood to falsehood, intrigue, and deceit."

Physically the Pushtoons appear to be of mixed Mediterranean type with many Nordic features, although any definitive conclusions must await further anthropometric study. It is safe to generalize that they are predominantly brunette whites, dolichocephalic [having a relatively long head], and of slender build with prominent facial features. Many are handsome by Western standards.

Origins of the Tadjiks

The second largest ethnic category in Afghanistan consists of the Tadjiks, who are scattered throughout the country but concentrated mainly in the north and west. Between two and three million Tadjiks live in Afghanistan; others live in Iran, the Soviet republic of Tadjikistan, and the Chinese province of Sinkiang. Although the Tadjiks are spoken of as a distinct group, recent investigation seems to indicate that they are actually several peoples who share no more than a name, a language (Persian), and sedentary living habits. Those in the west are often called Heratis, and probably have the same ancestry as the people of eastern Iran. Those north of the Hindu Kush are usually referred to as Parsiwans or Farsiwans ("Persian-speakers"); they show considerable Mongoloid admixture and are probably descended from a group of settlers from ancient Iran known as the Sarts. The "Mountain Tadjiks" described by Soviet ethnologists appear to have been among the earliest inhabitants of the region, and may indeed be autochthones [natives].

Tadjiks have few traditions about themselves or their origins, other than that they came from Arabia and derive their name from the Arabic word *taj* (for "ornament")—a sign that they were once "ornaments of the Prophet Mohammed." In fact, however, *Tadjik* is an Arabic term, which appears originally to have denoted a non-Arab Moslem, but which by the fourteenth century had come to mean a Persian-speaking sedentary Moslem—a definition that still fits the Tadjik well enough.

Tadjiks are not tribal, nor do they seem to have much pride in their ethnic identity, possibly because they have lived under the Pushtoon hegemony for two centuries. They are mainly agriculturists, often working as tenant farmers or laborers, although some are to be found engaged in trade or handicraft in Afghan cities. They are not belligerent except for the mountain Tadjiks of Kohistan, north of Kabul, who are considered to be as aggressive as Pushtoons.

The scanty anthropometric studies made thus far of the Tadjiks of Afghanistan indicate that they are brachycephalic [short-headed], and identify them with the Alpine division of the Caucasoid race. They are brunette whites and usually of slender build like the Pushtoons, but with more oval faces whose features appear less pronounced. As has been noted, many northern Tadjiks show traces of Mongoloid admixture. . . .

Uzbegs and Turkomen

In northern Afghanistan, between the Soviet border and the Hindu Kush, live approximately a million Afghans whose speech derives from the Ural-Altaic linguistic family. Of these by far the largest group are the Uzbegs [also spelled "Uzbeks"], who number about 800,000. Originally the name was applied to Turkic tribesmen who entered Afghanistan in the middle of the fifteenth century, one of whose early leaders was Uzbeg Khan, a descendant of the great [Mongol emperor] Genghis Khan. The Uzbegs of today are a mixture of these Turco-Mongols with the population of Iranian agriculturists whom they found in the area. Thus the modern Uzbegs have either Mongoloid or Caucasoid features or a blend of the two. They tend to be brachycephalic with yellow-white complexions and broad cheekbones, and occasionally with epicanthic eyefolds. They are more stocky in build than Pushtoons or Tadjiks, and some of them are corpulent, as the latter peoples seldom are.

The Uzbegs have given up the tribal affiliations and nomadism of their Turkic ancestors and are sedentary agriculturists, although some have become successful merchants and artisans. Their language, a form of Turkish called Uzbeki, apparently derives from the Chagataian Turkish of medieval times.

In Afghanistan the Uzbegs have a reputation, probably undeserved, for indolence and procrastination. They intermarry freely with their Tadjik neighbors but rarely with the Pushtoons, who consider them somewhat less than social equals. . . .

The other major Turkic group in Afghanistan, the Turkomen, number about 200,000 and are found mostly in the northwest. Most authorities believe they are descended from the Oghuz Turks who entered the area in the eleventh century, although they may have other strains in their ethnic background. They speak various Turkish dialects of a Western type.

Unlike the Uzbegs, the Turkomen are still pastoral, tribal nomads, the more important tribes being the Salor, Sariq, and

Tekke. They have few contacts with other Afghans and have had little importance in Afghan history. . . .

On the other hand, they have a distinct economic role as breeders of the karakul sheep, whose pelts—known as karakul, astrakhan, or Persian lamb—are the main Afghan export; and Turkomen women are weavers and dyers of the deep-red "Bokharan" rug which is another noted product. . . .

Religious Sects and Schisms

Any attempt to describe Afghan culture and customs in detail would be beyond the scope of this work. There are, however, certain fundamental aspects of that culture without which any understanding of Afghan history would be impossible. These are religion, tribalism, and the code of Pushtoon law known as Pushtoonwala.

Almost all Afghans are Moslems, Islam is the official creed of the country, and Islamic law, as interpreted by the system of Abu Hanifah,[2] is the legal code. Within Afghanistan, as in other pluralistic societies of Asia, Islam has been a major unifying force, whose traditions underlie Afghan folklore, literature and customs.

Probably about 80 per cent of all Afghans are members of the Sunni sect of Islam, which accepts the legitimacy of the four Khalifa or successors of the Prophet Mohammed. Most of the rest belong to the Ithna Ashariyah division of the Shia branch of Islam, which holds that Abu Bekr, Omar, and Othman were impostors and that the spiritual authority of Mohammed passed to his son-in-law Ali and thence to a line of imams or spiritual leaders. The Hazaras are Shia Moslems, as are the Turi Pushtoons, some clans of the Orakzai Pushtoons, and the Kizzilbash of Kabul.

This doctrinal difference, which has caused as much trouble in the lands of Islam as the controversy between Catholics and Protestants in the West, remains a divisive force in Afghanistan even though it has not produced the bloody confrontations that have occurred in other Moslem lands. Probably, however, it contributed to the hostility with which the Hazaras were regarded by their neighbors and the willingness of the Pushtoons to hold Hazara slaves; for the Pushtoons, unlike the Uzbegs, are inclined to consider the institution of slavery immoral. . . .

---

2. an early Islamic teacher and imam who founded a school of Islamic law

Tribe and Clan Loyalty

Tribes and tribalism are important in Afghanistan particularly among the Pushtoons, whose tribes vary in organization and in the degree of loyalty they command, but are strong and even at times divisive forces in the nation. Some of these tribes are large—the Yuzufzais, Durranis, and Ghilzais each have at least a million members—and others number no more than a few thousand. Of a multitude of terms denoting subdivisions four are commonly used: The *Ulus* or *Kaum* is the entire tribe. The *Khel* constitutes what might be called a subtribe, whose members live in the same general area. Next comes the clan, also called *Khel*, whose members live close together and often hold land in common. The smallest unit, the *Kor* or *Kahol*, is a family group whose members are all related.

The degree of loyalty to the tribe varies considerably. Among the Ghilzai, for example, it has been weakened by intertribal feuds and rivalries. On the other hand, the Durranis, even though they are divided into a number of subtribes and are dispersed over a wide territory, were able in the past to unite in a common cause—one reason for their hegemony over Afghanistan since its beginning as a nation.

The leaders of a tribe are known as *khans* or *maliks*—titles that are partly hereditary but can be won by outstanding individuals regardless of family. In some tribes the authority of such men is strong, and in others it is virtually nonexistent; but it is never absolute, and for any *khan* to adopt a policy not supported by the majority of his tribesmen would be both unusual and dangerous. Most tribal decisions are reached by a tribal *Jirga* or council, sometimes composed of *khans, maliks*, and elders, and sometimes of almost all the male members of the tribe. Some tribes, especially among the eastern Pushtoons, are so egalitarian that the decision of a *Jirga* is frequently defied by a tribesman supported by a numerous and powerful family.

Living with the tribes are a number of nontribesmen known as *hamsayah*—a word literally meaning "neighbor" but more exactly rendered in this connection as "client." These people have an inferior social position and take no part in tribal decisions, but they are under the protection of their hosts and any offense to them would be avenged no less stringently, or in some cases, even more so, than if they had been tribesmen.

Among the tribes and throughout Afghanistan as a whole, the

most important unit is the extended family, which for any individual comprises all relatives by blood or marriage. Theoretically the oldest male is its dominant member, but in practice the position may be taken by anyone of accepted ability or position, and sometimes by a woman. Interfamily rivalries and hatreds exist, particularly in situations complicated by plural marriages and antagonistic half brothers but any instance of need places all members of a family under strong social pressure to render assistance. This includes economic necessity, and Afghans who as a result of illness, injury or any other cause cannot earn a living are certain of support by the affluent members of the extended family.

The Pushtoon Code

Undoubtedly the strongest determinant of the ethnic character of the Pushtoon Afghans, and an influence on non-Pushtoons to some degree, is the code of custom known as *Pushtoonwala* or the "law of the Pushtoons." It covers three separate injunctions: *nanawatai* (literally, "I have come in"), or sanctuary; *badal*, or retaliation; and *mailmasti*, or hospitality. *Nanawatai* calls for protection to be extended to anyone, even an enemy, in search of refuge, and for mediation on behalf of a person wishing to make peace with someone he has injured. Its most extreme form occurs when a woman sends her veil to a man, imploring his assistance for herself or her family; to ignore such an appeal would be almost unthinkable. *Nanawatai* is declining in importance, but is still powerful among the tribes. . . .

Badal calls for revenge or retaliation for injury or insult to oneself or to a member of one's family. The nature of this retribution varies among the tribes; in some it can be settled by money payment or the intercession of elders, and in others only personal vengeance will suffice. The variation, incidentally, is not proportionate to the sophistication of the tribesmen. The Waziris and Mahsuds, probably the fiercest of Pushtoon tribesmen, are often willing to accept a money payment, and in any event will direct their anger at the specific offender. The far more sophisticated Afridis, on the other hand, usually insist on personal revenge, and regard all members of the offender's family as equally involved.

Personal retaliation with its concomitant of blood feuds has been practiced in many places, but in few as scrupulously as among the Pushtoon Afghans. Like the concept of the extended family, it arose from the need for protection in lands where law-enforcement agencies were absent, and it still acts as a deterrent upon predatory behavior. But it also encourages feuds and enmities which may last for generations, and is one of the reasons why the Pushtoon people, for all their pride of ethnic identity, have found unity so difficult. Naturally it has declined wherever the Afghan government has established law and order, but it is still real enough that Afghans, generally even those of the urban and educated classes, take any insult, injury, or slight with extreme seriousness.

Mailmasti, or hospitality, among some of the tribes, is considered almost a sacred duty. To an Afghan the person and property of a guest are inviolable, and his comfort and pleasure are the host's chief concern. Quite possibly the Afghans are the most hospitable people in the world; no one is more despised than a niggardly host, and to invite away a guest in another's house is literally a mortal insult. As a social imperative, the open-handed hospitality found throughout Afghanistan is almost absolute.

Pushtoonwala is fading as Afghanistan replaces tribal loyalty with nationalism. Nevertheless, it remains a powerful force in the behavior of Afghans, including both the non-Pushtoons who are outside its provisions and the city-dwellers who have discarded their ethnic affiliations.

No brief summary can do justice to the complexity of Afghan customs. By way of generalization, it may be said that the cultures of India, Iran, and Turan are all reflected to a degree in that of Afghanistan. The heaviest influence is that of Iran and the Middle East; somewhat less important is the culture of India, and still less so is that of the Turanians to the north. To all of the cultural patterns thus adopted the Afghans, and above all the Pushtoons, have added their unique stamp, to produce an Asian nation unlike any other.

Early Conquests

BY SALLY ANN BAYNARD

Afghanistan lies across the pivotal land routes between the Indian subcontinent, Iran, and central Asia. In ancient times, many people migrated through the Afghanistan region and often settled there, creating a rich culture shaped by many ethnicities and language groups. Afghanistan's strategic location has also made it an area of conflict and conquest. In the following selection, Sally Ann Baynard describes the succession of the earliest rulers who conquered the area that would become modern-day Afghanistan, including Alexander the Great, the Seleucids, the Kushans, and the White Huns, or Hepthalites. Baynard also details the slow Muslim conquest of the area that began with the first Arab raid on Kandahar in 700. Islam soon dominated the region, and soon after the Mongol ruler Genghis Khan invaded central Asia in 1220, his appointed governors adopted Islam and became practicing Muslims. Sally Ann Baynard is an adjunct professor in the School of Foreign Service at Georgetown Public Policy Institute in Washington, D.C.

T he area that is present-day Afghanistan comprised several satrapies (provinces) of the Achaemenid Empire[1] at its most extensive under [Persian ruler] Darius the Great (ca. 500 B.C.). The Iranians had subdued these areas to the east with only the greatest difficulty, however, and had to keep substantial garrisons in some of the satrapies in the Hindu Kush areas. Bactriana, with its capital at Bactria (which later became Balkh), was reputedly the home of [Iranian prophet] Zoroaster, who founded the religion that bears his name.

By the fourth century B.C., Iranian control of outlying areas and the internal cohesion of the empire had become tenuous. Although such areas as Bactriana had always been restless under

---

1. A Persian empire led by the Achaemenid dynasty, whose rulers included Cyrus II the Great, Darius the Great, and Xerxes I. The last Achaemenid ruler was Darius III, who was defeated in 330 B.C. by Alexander III of Macedon.

Sally Ann Baynard, "Historical Setting," in *Afghanistan: A Country Study*, ed. Richard F. Nyrop and Donald M. Seekins. Washington, DC: U.S. Government Printing Office, 1986.

Achaemenid rule, there were Bactrian troops at the decisive Battle of Gaugamela (330 B.C.) fighting on the side of the Iranians, who were defeated by [Macedonian conqueror] Alexander the Great.

Alexander and Greek Rule

It took Alexander three years, about 330–327 B.C., to subdue the areas that now make up Afghanistan and adjacent areas in the Soviet Union. Moving eastward from the area of Herat, the Macedonian leader encountered fierce resistance from local rulers who had been satraps of the Iranians. Alexander overwhelmed local resistance and even married Roxane, a daughter of the satrap of Bactriana. In 327 B.C. Alexander entered the Indian subcontinent, where the progress of his conquest was stopped only by a mutiny of his troops. Although his expedition through what is now Afghanistan was brief, he left behind a Hellenic cultural influence that lasted several centuries.

Upon Alexander's death in 323 B.C., his empire, never politically consolidated, broke apart. His cavalry commander, Seleucus, took nominal control of the eastern lands and founded the Seleucid Dynasty. Under the Seleucids, as under Alexander, Greek colonists and soldiers came to the region of the Hindu Kush, and many are believed to have remained. At the same time the Mauryan Empire was developing in the northern part of the Indian subcontinent, and it managed, beginning about 30 years after Alexander's death, to take control of the southeasternmost areas of the Seleucid domains, including parts of what is now Afghanistan. The Mauryans introduced Indic culture, including Buddhism, into the area. With the Seleucids on one side and the Mauryans on the other, the people of the Hindu Kush were in what would become a familiar position in modern as well as ancient history, i.e., between two empires.

The Seleucids were unable to hold the contentious eastern area of their domain, and in the middle of the third century B.C. an independent, Greek-ruled state was declared in Bactria. With the decline of even nominal Seleucid control, the period from shortly after the death of Alexander until the middle of the second century saw a variety of Greek dynasties ruling out of Bactria. The farthest extent of Graeco-Bactrian rule came in about 170 B.C., when it included most of the territory that is now between the Iranian deserts and the Ganges River and from Central Asia to the Arabian Sea. Graeco-Bactrian rule fell prey to the internecine disputes that plagued Greek rulers to the west, to ambitious attempts to extend control into northern India, and to pressure from two groups of nomadic invaders from Central Asia—the Parthians and Sakas (perhaps the Seythians). Greek civilization left few, if any, permanent effects, whereas characteristics of Iranian civilization were accepted and retained by the peoples of the Hindu Kush.

Central Asian and Sassanian Rule

The third and second centuries B.C. witnessed the advent to the Iranian Plateau of nomadic people speaking Indo-European languages. The Parthians established control in most of what is now Iran as early as the middle of the third century B.C., and about 100 years later another Indo-European group—either the Sakas or the Kushans (a subgroup of the tribe called the Yueh-chih by the Chinese)—entered what is now Afghanistan and established an empire that lasted almost four centuries. The Kushans, whose empire was among the most powerful of its time, were pushed into the Hindu Kush area by the Hsiungnu (Huns) of Central Asia, who had themselves been thwarted in their attacks on China by the powerful Han Dynasty.

The Kushan Empire spread from the valley of the Kabul River to defeat other Central Asian tribes that had conquered parts of the northern central Iranian Plateau that had been ruled by the Parthians. By the middle of the first century B.C. the Kushans controlled the area from the Indus Valley to the Gobi Desert and as far west as the central part of the Iranian Plateau. Early in the second century A.D. under Kanishka, the greatest of the Kushan rulers, the empire reached its greatest geographic extent and became a center of literature and art. Kanishka spread Kushan control to the mouth of the Indus River, into Kashmir, and into what are now the Chinese-controlled areas north of Tibet. Although details of his rule are fragmentary, Kanishka is believed to have ruled from a capital not far from present-day Peshawar, with a summer residence at Kapisa, north of what is now Kabul. Kanishka was a patron of the arts and religious learning. It was during his reign that Mahayana Buddhism, brought to Northern India earlier by the Mauryan emperor Asoka (ca. 260–232 B.C.) reached its peak in Central Asia. The Kushan Empire was a center of trade, especially in silk, and the Buddhism of its rulers followed trade routes into East Asia, with which Kanishka and his successors maintained commercial relations.

In the third century A.D. Kushan control degenerated into independent kingdoms that were easy targets for conquest by the
rising Iranian dynasty, the Sassanians (ca. 224–561 A.D.). Although
the Sassanians conquered as far east as the Punjab, by the middle
of the third century most of the kingdoms that were fragments
of the Kushan Empire were in practice semi-independent. These
small kingdoms were pressed not only by the Sassanians from the
west but also from the Indian subcontinent by the growing
strength of the Guptas, a dynasty established in northern and central India as early as the beginning of the fourth century.

DEFINING JIHAD

When Muslim warriors in the ninth century began to spread the re-
ligion of Islam to what is now Afghanistan, one of their missions
was to promote jihad, or holy war. In this excerpt, journalist Ahmed
Rashid argues that the higher purpose of jihad is to encourage fol-
lowers' efforts to improve themselves.

In Western thought, heavily influenced by the medieval
Christian Crusaders—with their own ideas about "holy
war"—jihad has always been portrayed as an Islamic war
against unbelievers. Westerners point to the conquest of
Spain in the eighth century by the Moors and the vast Ottoman Empire of the thirteen through twentieth centuries,
and focus on the bloodshed, ignoring not only the enormous
achievements in science and art and the basic tolerance of
these empires, but also the true idea of jihad that spread
peacefully throughout these realms. Militancy is not the
essence of jihad.

The greater jihad as explained by The Prophet Muhammad is first inward-seeking: it involves the effort of each
Muslim to become a better human being, to struggle to improve him- or herself. In doing so the follower of jihad can
also benefit his or her community. In addition, jihad is a test
of each Muslim's obedience to God and willingness to implement His commands on earth. As [scholar] Barbara Met-

The disunited Kushan and Sassanian kingdoms were in a bad position to meet the threat of a new wave of nomadic, Indo-European invaders from the north. The Hepthalites (or White Huns) swept out of Central Asia in the fourth or fifth century into Bactria and the areas to the south, overwhelming the last of the Kushan-Sassanian kingdoms. Although little is known of these people—as is the case with most of the pre-Islamic, Central Asian invaders of the Hindu Kush area—it is believed that their control lasted about a century and was marked by constant warfare with the Sassanians to the west.

calf described it, "Jihad is the inner struggle of moral discipline and commitment to Islam and political action." It is also true that Islam sanctions rebellion against an unjust ruler, whether Muslim or not, and jihad can become the means to mobilize that political and social struggle. This is the lesser jihad. Thus, Muslims revere the life of The Prophet Muhammad because it exemplified both the greater and the lesser jihad—The Prophet struggled lifelong to improve Himself as a Muslim in order both to set an example to those around Him and to demonstrate His complete commitment to God. But He also fought against the corrupt Arab society He was living in, and He used every means—including but not exclusively militant ones—to transform it.

Today's global jihadi movements, from the Taliban in Afghanistan to Osama bin Laden's worldwide Al Qaeda to the Islamic Movement of Uzbekistan (IMU), ignore the greater jihad advocated by The Prophet and adopt the lesser jihad as a complete political and social philosophy. Yet nowhere in Muslim writings or tradition does jihad sanction the killing of innocent non-Muslim men, women, and children, or even fellow Muslims, on the basis of ethnicity, sect, or belief. It is this perversion of jihad—as a justification to slaughter the innocent—which in part defines the radical new fundamentalism of today's most extreme Islamic movements.

Ahmed Rashid, *Jihad: The Rise of Militant Islam in Central Asia.* New York: Penguin, 2002, pp. 1–2.

Buddhist and Zoroastrian Cultures

By the middle of the sixth century, at the latest, the Hepthalites were defeated in the territories north of the Amu Darya (in present-day Soviet Union) by another group of Central Asian nomads, the Western Turks, and by the resurgent Sassanians in the lands south of the Amu Darya (frequently cited in old texts as the Oxus River). Up to the advent of Islam, the lands of the Hindu Kush were dominated up to the Amu Darya by small kingdoms under general Sassanian overlordship but with local rulers who were Kushan or Hepthalite.

In the mid–seventh century, in the last years before the end of Buddhist and Zoroastrian cultures in the area, a Chinese pilgrim, Hsuan Tsang, passed through Balkh to India. Historian W. Kerr Fraser-Tytler recounts Hsuan Tsang's findings:

> He found in the north a Turkish ruler . . . a devout Buddhist who treated his revered guest with kindness and sent him to visit Balkh before starting on his difficult journey across the mountains. At Balkh Hsuan Tsang found that, in spite of the ravages of the Ephthalites, there were still a hundred monasteries in and around a city lying amid fertile lands and valleys, where today there is only desolation and arid waste. He crossed the Hindu Kush and . . . reached Bamiyan, at that time a flourishing community, including ten monasteries in that high beautiful valley in the heart of the mountains through which all the caravans from China passed on their journey down to India. . . . He reached Kapisa . . . and there found a Turkish (or Ephthalite) ruler whose dominion extended as far as the Indus and who, commanding as he did the main trade routes to India, was of sufficient importance to send a present of horses, for which the country was then famous, to the Son of Heaven, the Emperor T'ai-tsung, and to receive presents in exchange. Thence the pilgrim passed . . . into India, noting . . . the contrast between the fierce tribesmen of the mountains and the more effeminate Indians of the lower valleys.

Of this great Buddhist culture and earlier Zoroastrian civilization there remain few, if any, traces in the life of the people of Afghanistan. On the ancient trade routes, however, there are still stone monuments of Buddhist culture. Two great sandstone Buddhas, 35 and 53 meters high and dating from the third and fifth centuries A.D., overlook the ancient route through Bamian to Balkh.[2] In this area and other spots within what is now Afghanistan, archaeologists have found frescoes, stucco decorations, statuary, and rare objects from China, Rome, and Phoenicia that were made as early as the second century A.D. and that bear witness to the richness of the ancient civilizations of the area.

Islamic Conquest

In 637 A.D., only five years after the death of the Prophet Muhammad, the Arab Muslims shattered the might of the Iranian Sassanians at the battle of Qadisiya, and the invaders began to reach into the lands east of Iran. The Muslim conquest was a prolonged struggle in the area that is now Afghanistan. Following the first Arab raid into Qandahar in about 700, local rulers, probably either Kushans or Western Turks, began to come under the control of Ummayid caliphs, who sent Arab military governors and tax collectors into the region. By the middle of the eighth century the rising Abbasid Dynasty was able to subdue the area. There was a period of peace under the rule of the caliph, Harun al Rashid (785–809), and his son, in which learning flourished in such Central Asian cities as Samarkand, located in what is now the Soviet Union. Over the period of the seventh through the ninth centuries, most inhabitants of what is now Afghanistan, Pakistan, the southern parts of the Soviet Union, and some of northern India were converted to Sunni Islam, which replaced the Zorastrianism, Hinduism, Buddhism, and indigenous religions of previous empires.

During the eighth and ninth centuries, partly to obtain better grazing land, ancestors of many of the Turkic-speaking groups now identifiable in Afghanistan settled in the Hindu Kush area. Some of these tribes settled in what are now Ghor, Ghazni, and Kabul provinces and began to assimilate much of the culture and language of the already present Pashtun tribes.

By the middle of the ninth century, Abbasid rule had faltered, and semi-independent states began to emerge throughout the empire. In the Hindu Kush area three short-lived, local dynasties emerged. The best known of the three, the Sammanid, ruling out

2. These Buddha statues were destroyed by the Taliban in 2001.

of Bukhara (in what is now the Soviet Union), extended its rule briefly as far east as India and west into Iran. Bukhara and neighboring Samarkand were centers of science, the arts and Islamic studies. Although Arab Muslim intellectual life still centered on Baghdad, Iranian Muslim scholarship, i.e., Shia Islam, at this time predominated in the Sammanid areas. By the mid–tenth century the Sammanid Dynasty crumbled in the face of attack from the Turkish tribes to the north and from a rising dynasty to the south, the Ghaznavids.

Ghaznavid and Ghorid Rule

Out of the Sammanid Dynasty came the first great Islamic empire in Afghanistan, the Ghaznavid, whose warriors raided deep into the Indian subcontinent and at the same time assured the domination of Sunni Islam in what is now Afghanistan, Pakistan, and parts of India. In the middle of the tenth century Alptigin, a Turkish slave warrior of the Sammanid garrison in Nishapur (in present-day Iran), failed in a coup attempt against his masters and fled with his followers to Ghazni, which became the capital of the empire ruled by his successors. The most renowned among them was Mahmud, who consolidated control over the areas south of the Amu Darya, then carried out devastating raids into India, looting Hindu temples and seeking converts to Islam. With his booty from India he built a great capital at Ghazni, founded universities, and patronized scholars, such as historians Al Biruni and Al Utbi, and the poet Firdawsi. Mahmud was recognized by the caliph in Baghdad as the temporal heir of the Sammanids. By the time of his death, Mahmud ruled all the Hindu Kush area and as far east as the Punjab, as well as territories well north of the Amu Darya.

As occurred so often in this region, the death of the military genius who extended the empire to its farthest extent was the death knell of the empire itself. Mahmud died in 1130, and the Seljuk Turks, also Muslims by this time, attacked the Ghaznavid empire from the north and west, while the rulers of the kingdom of Ghor, southeast of Herat, captured and burnt Ghazni, just as the Ghaznavids had once conquered Ghor. Not until 1186, however, was the last representative of the Ghaznavid Dynasty uprooted by the Ghorids from his holdout in the Punjab.

By 1200 Turkish dynasties were in power in all of the easternmost areas of the Abbasid empire, whose caliph was, by this time, a ruler in name only. The Ghorids controlled most of what is now Afghanistan, eastern Iran, and Pakistan, while parts of central and western Iran were ruled by Seljuk Turks (who would eventually sweep all the way to what is now Turkey). Around 1200 most Ghorid lands came into the hands of the Khwarazm Turks, who had invaded from Central Asia across the Amu Darya.

The Great Invaders

By Martin Ewans

Afghanistan's extremely mountainous terrain has always made travel in the region difficult. Nevertheless, because of its strategic location at the crossroads of central Asia and the Indian subcontinent, many empires have sought to conquer Afghanistan throughout its history. In the fourth century, the Macedonian king Alexander the Great invaded the land and founded cities there. Other invaders also conquered Afghanistan, including Huns, Kushans, and Muslim Arabs. Each group left its imprint on the area's politics, religion, art, and culture.

In the following selection, historian Martin Ewans describes the invasion of warrior Genghis Khan and his Mongol followers in the thirteenth century, which left the area in ruins. Ewans also details the subsequent invasions by two other famous conquerors: Tamerlane, a Turko-Mongol who created an empire that included Afghanistan and northern India, and Mohammed Zahir-ud-din, more commonly known as Babur. Martin Ewans is a former officer of the British diplomatic service who served in many countries, including Afghanistan, Pakistan, and India. He is the chairman of Children's Aid Direct, an international charity.

There occurred [in the early 1200s] one of the most cataclysmic events of Afghan history, the invasion of the Mongol hordes under their chieftain Genghis Khan. The latter was a brilliant military commander and administrator, who founded an empire that eventually stretched from Hungary to the China Sea and from northern Siberia to the Persian Gulf and the Indian sub-continent. The origins of his followers are still a matter of dispute, the most likely theory being that they were descendants of the Hsiung-Nu. Genghis Khan's achievement was to weld them into a formidable fighting force, distinguished by its superb cavalry, which was capable of highly disciplined manoeuvre and sustained advance at great speed, even over near-impossible terrain. Genghis Khan himself started life

Martin Ewans, *Afghanistan: A Short History of Its People and Politics.* New York: HarperCollins Publishers, 2002. Copyright © 2002 by Martin Ewans. Reproduced by permission of the publisher.

as an abandoned orphan, but managed after many vicissitudes to attract support to the point where, in 1206, he was proclaimed emperor of a Mongol confederation, probably some two million strong. In 1218, out of the blue, he and his followers descended on Turkestan, defeated the Khwarizm Shahs and took Bokhara and Samarkand, which they comprehensively sacked. In 1221 they took Balkh, razed it to the ground and massacred its inhabitants. When the Taoist seer and healer, Ch'ang Ch'un, who had been summoned from China to Genghis' court in Afghanistan, arrived at the city a short while after the massacre, he found that the citizens had been 'removed', but 'we could still hear dogs barking in its streets'. The Mongols treated Herat leniently when it first surrendered to them, but when it rebelled six months later, it was speedily retaken and all its inhabitants were executed, the process taking seven days to complete. Bamian was also razed and its population slaughtered, leaving today only the ruins of two hilltop fortresses, the Shahr-i-Zohak (Red City) and the aptly named Shahr-i-Gholgola (City of Sighs) as evidence of the calamity. Ghazni then suffered the same fate, as did Peshawar, but Genghis Khan did not advance beyond the Punjab, probably nervous of the effect on his army of the heat of the Indian plains. The overall outcome of the Mongol invasion was widespread depopulation, devastation and economic ruin. When the Moroccan traveller, Ibn Batuta, passed through Afghanistan a century later, he found Balkh in ruins and uninhabited, Kabul no more than a village and Ghazni devastated. He reports Genghis Khan as having torn down the mosque at Balkh, 'one of the most beautiful in the world', because he believed that treasure had been hidden beneath one of its columns.

Tamerlane

Following Genghis Khan's death in 1227, his sons and grandsons ruled his empire, most of Afghanistan coming under his second son, Jaghatai, whose descendants established themselves in Kabul and Ghazni. Herat alone retained a degree of autonomy under a Tajik dynasty [the Tajiks are one of Afghanistan's major ethnic groups], the Karts. From 1364 onwards, the western part of the khanate came under the control of Tamerlane (a corruption of *Timur-i-Leng*—Timur the Lame), a Turko-Mongol who claimed, apparently falsely, descent from Genghis himself. Tamerlane began by expelling the Mongols from Transoxania and around 1370 proclaimed himself emperor at Balkh. He too went on to create an extensive empire, which included Afghanistan and northern India, and in 1398 he took Delhi and slaughtered its inhabitants. Among his unpleasant habits was that of stacking into pyramids the heads of those he had massacred or incorporating them into walls. In the Sistan, he destroyed the irrigation works that stemmed from the Helmand River, with the result that what had been a prosperous and well-inhabited region was turned into a desert waste. The weathered remains of substantial towns and fortresses even today provide clear evidence of the scale of the destruction, from which Sistan never recovered. However, unlike Genghis Khan, Tamerlane was, despite his barbaric propensities, a man of culture, and he transformed the Timurid capital, Samarkand, into an intellectual and artistic centre. His tomb there is one of the glories of Islamic architecture. His empire began to disintegrate after his death in 1405, but his dynasty, the Timurids, continued to rule in Turkestan and Persia until the early sixteenth century. Under his son, Shah Rukh, Herat became the centre of what has been called the Timurid Renaissance, with a thriving culture notable for its architecture, its literary and musical achievements, and its calligraphy and miniature painting. Shah Rukh's formidable wife, Gohar Shad, was responsible for the building of the Musalla, the complex of mosque, college and mausoleum which, with its several minarets, dominated the Herat skyline over many centuries. The bulk of it was razed at the time of the Panjdeh crisis in 1885, to create a clear field of fire for the defenders of the city, in the event, thought to be imminent, of a Russian attack from the north. Of the minarets which were left, [historian] Robert Byron says, in his encomium of Timurid architecture,

> Their beauty is more than scenic, depending on light and landscape. On closer view, every tile, every flower, every petal of mosaic contributes its genius to the whole. Even in ruin, such architecture tells of a golden age. . . . The few travellers who have visited Samarkhand and Bokhara as well as the shrine of the Imam Riza [in Meshed], say that nothing in these towns can equal the last. If they are right, the Mosque of Gohar Shad must be the greatest surviving monument of the period, while the ruins of Herat show that there was once a greater.

Babur

The Timurid Renaissance lasted little more than a century. Following Shah Rukh's death in 1447, ten successive rulers held Herat over a period of a mere twelve years, but it was then taken by another Timurid, Husain-i-Baiqara, who gave it a further forty years of peace and a renewed cultural flowering. The miniature painter Bihzad, the poet Abdurrahman Jami and the historian Mishkwand all embellished his court. Then, during the sixteenth century, two new dynasties began to impinge on Afghanistan. In Persia, the Safavids presided over a national renaissance and survived until well into the eighteenth century, despite conflicts with the Ottoman Turks and the Usbeks, who had moved south into the region around 1500. Also at the turn of the sixteenth century, a descendant of both Tamerlane and Genghis Khan, Mohammed Zahir-ud-din, better known as Babur, assumed power in Kabul and Ghazni. Babur came originally from Ferghana, a small khanate some two hundred miles east of Samarkand. His father having died in a landslip while feeding his pigeons on the wall of his palace, Babur, while still in his teens, conceived the ambition of conquering Samarkand. In 1497, after a seven months' siege, he took the city, but his supporters gradually deserted him and Ferghana was taken from him in his absence. Within a few months he was compelled to retire from Samarkand, and for the next few years he and a small band of followers survived only by living a freebooting existence. Eventually he retook Samarkand, but was again forced out, this time by an Usbek leader, Shaibani Khan, who also took Herat. Once more reduced to destitution, Babur decided in 1504 to trek over the Hindu Kush to Kabul, where the current ruler promptly retreated to Kandahar and left him in undisputed control of the city. Babur became extremely fond of Kabul, and proceeded to settle down and indulge one of his great pleasures, the construction of gardens. In his memoirs, he gives a vivid account of the great ebb and flow of trade which passed through Kabul at that time, but which was later to decline as the sea routes to India were developed. The city, he recorded, was

> an excellent and profitable market for commodities. . . .
> Every year seven, eight or ten thousand horses arrive in
> Kabul. From Hindustan every year fifteen, twenty
> thousand pieces of cloth are brought by caravans. The
> commodities of Hindustan are slaves, white cloths,

> sugar candy, refined and common sugar, drugs and
> spices. There are many merchants who are not satisfied
> with getting three or four hundred per cent.

In 1511, Babur again took Samarkand, but yet again was driven out, so that he finally abandoned his ambitions in that direction and turned towards India. He gradually established his ascendancy over the neighbouring Pushtoon tribes, captured Kandahar and acquired artillery, employing a Turkish gunner to operate it. After several probing raids, he finally launched a full scale invasion of India in 1525 and defeated the Lodi kings, themselves an Afghan dynasty, who had ruled in Delhi since 1451. In 1527 he went on to defeat the Rajputs at Khanua, west of Agra, and established himself at the latter city as the founder of the dynasty of the Great Moguls which was to rule India with glittering magnificence over the following two centuries.

Like Mahmud of Ghazni and Tamerlane, Babur combined military prowess with cultural sophistication. He was an accomplished poet in both Persian and Turkic and was a sensitive observer of nature. Many pages of his memoirs, which he wrote over a period of some forty years, are devoted to the flora and fauna of both Afghanistan and India, and his love of gardening shines through at every turn. His writings also show him to have been a man of great charm, intelligence and humanity. His description of the Timurid court of Husain-i-Baiqara is invaluable as a picture of the age. His judgment of men is sensitive and acute. However, until somewhat late in life, he was also a hard drinker and his health was never good, particularly while he was in India. He died in 1530 and was later buried in Kabul, where his tomb still stands in a garden that he created.

Ahmad Khan and the Durrani Empire

By Stephen Tanner

In the sixteenth century Afghan tribesmen began to adopt the newest weapons available at that time, including cannons and, later, matchlocks and muskets. With these new technologies and their warrior heritage, the tribesmen began to dominate the more sedentary peoples living on the frontiers of the Hindu Kush Mountains. In the following selection, Stephen Tanner describes how one young Afghan leader, Ahmad Khan, later called Ahmad Shah, began to unify the unruly Afghan tribes. In 1747 Ahmad Shah and his fellow warriors began more than two decades of invasions into neighboring India and Persia (now Iran) to acquire lands and goods. Eventually, Shah's Durrani Empire included all of modern Afghanistan, most of modern Pakistan, the province of Kashmir, and parts of India and Iran. Tanner argues that Ahmad Shah shaped Afghanistan into a strong and independent political entity. However, when the Afghan ruler died in 1772, the empire entered a decline and began to lose the lands it had conquered. Stephen Tanner is a military historian and freelance writer. He is the author of Afghanistan: A Military History from Alexander the Great to the Fall of the Taliban.

In 1747 near Kandahar [a city in Afghanistan], the Abdali tribes held a council, or *jirga*, to choose their next leader. Ahmad Khan, then barely twenty-five, was the youngest of the candidates, and according to some accounts the least active in pressing his case. Yet a holy man, Sabir Khan, announced that Ahmad was the greatest man among them and placed a sheaf of wheat on his head as a symbolic crown. The tribal leaders acquiesced in the choice partly because Ahmad was from the small Saddozai sub-tribe of the Abdalis and would thus be unlikely to upset larger rivalries, and partly because he had already proven himself a skilled commander. The holy man pronounced him Ahmad Shah "Durr-i-Durran," or "Pearl of Pearls." The Abdalis thenceforward called themselves Durranis.

Just days after assuming his new title, Ahmad Shah (neé Khan) received a great stroke of fortune when a richly laden caravan lumbered into Kandahar from India, unaware that Nadir Shah [Shah of Persia] had been killed. Ahmad seized the treasure and spread much of it among his followers, consolidating his support. The Ghilzais [a tribe of western Afghanistan], who had been cut to ribbons during the last stages of their Persian venture, were willing to go along with Durrani leadership. The combined tribes then embarked on a quarter century of plunder. . . .

Into India and Persia

After establishing his capital at Kandahar, Ahmad Shah led his forces north to seize Ghazni and Kabul. The latter had been held by a Persian governor, who after Nadir Shah's death, tried to switch his allegiance to the Moghuls [Muslim rulers of north India]; finding no help there either, he simply surrendered to the advancing Afghans. Ahmad then led his forces into the Punjab, seeking to reclaim the territories once ceded by the Moghuls to Nadir Shah. East of the Indus, however, his 12,000-man cavalry army was defeated at the battle of Manupur by a larger Moghul force under a general named Mir Mannu.

The following year, the Afghans returned and seized Lahore [in Pakistan]. Unwilling to wage a major war on their northern frontier, the Moghuls formally ceded the Punjab. Ahmad Shah allowed Mir Mannu to remain as governor of the territory with the task of forwarding tax revenues. On his return to Afghanistan, Ahmad Shah picked up new supporters from the eastern tribes, and after reassembling his forces at Kandahar led 25,000 men against Herat. This oft-contested city—the easternmost of Persia's Khorasan and westernmost of the Afghan tribes—was finally taken after a nine-month siege.

The Durranis then proceeded to the Persian capital, Mashhad, which was then ruled by Shah Rukh, a sixteen-year-old grandson of Nadir Shah, who had earlier been blinded by a rival. It is possible that Ahmad had known Shah Rukh when he was a small boy, and in any event seemed to have some affection for him. After a short siege, the Afghans took the capital, but Ahmad allowed Shah Rukh to remain in office. Farther west at Nisha-pur, however, the Afghans were bloodily repulsed and had to re-group at Herat.

The following spring Ahmad Shah returned to Nishapur, this time with heavy artillery. His largest cannon, cast and assembled during the siege, blew up the first time it was fired, but its 500-pound missile created such havoc in the city that Nishapur promptly surrendered. Still stung from their previous defeat, the Afghans ravaged populace, killing many citizens and enslaving others. The blind young Shah Rukh had meanwhile rebelled in Khorasan; however, after quashing the revolt Ahmad Shah once again let the young man keep his throne on the promise that he would consider his domain part of the Durrani Empire. At this time, Ahmad Shah also sent a mobile force into northern Afghanistan to seize Balkh, Mazar-i-Sharif (which had become more important), Taliqan, Kunduz, and other cities from the Uzbeks, Tajiks, and Turkmen who had drifted south of the Oxus.

While Ahmad Shah had been occupied in the west, Mir Mannu had raised the Punjab [mountainous region of northern India] again on behalf of the Moghuls, and in 1752 the Durra-nis recrossed the Indus. This time they secured their hold on La-hore and Multan, and with the help of the Yuzufzai border tribe conquered Kashmir. The Moghul emperor once again forswore any claim on revenue from his western provinces and sealed the bargain by paying an enormous sum of tax arrears to make the Durranis go away. The curious system of Moghul governance of the Punjab on behalf of the Durranis took on an absurd aspect when Mir Mannu died in 1753 and the Moghul emperor named his own three-year-old son as the new governor, with Mir Mannu's two-year-old as his vizier. Real power was held by Mir Mannu's widow, who made an utter mess of things ruling from her scandal-ridden bedroom. In 1757 Ahmad Shah returned, and this time marched all the way to Delhi. He allowed the new Moghul emperor, Alamgir, to retain his throne on the condition that he recognize Durrani sovereignty over not only the Punjab but Kashmir and Sind.

Fighting the Marathas

To the Afghans at this time, the problem in India was no longer the Moghuls, who were at least fellow Muslims, but the energetic Marathas, who had been able to harness the latent power of the vast Hindu population into a seemingly unstoppable tide from the south. From their capital at Poona in east-central India, the Marathas had overrun much of the Deccan and were now expanding north. Beginning in late 1759, the Afghans vied with them for over a year, unable to stop them from seizing Delhi.

In 1761 Ahmad Shah marched from Kandahar and crossed the Indus for the fifth time, to face the Maratha army at Panipat, the traditional battleground for contesting the rule of northern India. The sides were evenly matched with seventy to eighty thousand men apiece and for a few hours the outcome hung in the balance. But then Ahmad Shah himself led a counterattack that collapsed the Maratha center, prompting a wholesale massacre of the enemy army and its horde of camp followers. This battle had enormous consequences, for if a powerful Hindu state had been able

LOYA JIRGA: THE AFGHAN COUNCIL

The loya jirga, *or grand council, has long been a part of Afghan society and is still important today. The following excerpt briefly describes the* loya jirga's *history and function.*

In Pashto, the word *Loya* means great and *Jirga* stands for council or meeting. *Loya Jirga* has been used as a political instrument for finding solutions to issues of great national importance in Afghanistan.

It is a fact that for as long as history remembers, human societies in their long historical evolution have used councils and meetings to decide on issues that directly impacted their lives within their families, villages, tribes and regions. Even prehistoric man used councils in deciding how to deal with the wild that threatened his life or how to deal with natural calamities or even hostile neighboring tribes. . . .

The Afghan tradition from the pre-Islamic times contained the provision for councils. This was especially so because of the tribal nature of the Afghan society. The economic base of the population, mainly agriculture and livestock breeding, together with the need for migratory herdsmen who had to to establish itself in India, encroachments by seafaring Europeans would have been far more difficult, if possible at all. Instead, the Marathas had been crippled, the Moghuls were no longer of much use, and the Afghans, disinclined in any case to tolerate the climate south of Delhi, stockpiled all their talents into fighting instead of governance. The suppression of the Maratha surge also allowed a new group to gain power in the Punjab—the Sikhs.

At its height in 1762, the Durrani Empire encompassed all of modern Afghanistan plus Iran's Khorasan, nearly all of modern Pakistan, part of India, and the province of Kashmir. It stretched from the Amu Darya in the north to the Arabian Sea in the south. The southern regions were gained more through an alliance with the Brahui and Baluch tribes than through conquest across those wastelands.

---

travel for pasture with the seasons, and lack of efficient communication systems, all contributed to a dire need for consultation in the forms of intra and intertribal gatherings. All Afghan tribes, including the Pashtoons, Tajiks, Uzbeks, the Hazaras, the Nooris, the Turkemens, the Baloochis and all other minor ethnic groups, have traditionally had a mechanism of consultation in the form of local, regional and national assemblies. When these meetings were held within the tribes, they decided issues such as water rights, the rights of individuals within families, mediating peace between feuding clans, face saving in cases that involved violation of individual or family honors, and settling other feuds such as vengeances or settling sanguine issues in cases of murders, marriages, divorces etc. In its intertribal form, the councils reached agreements on water rights, land borders, right to pastures, trade, tribal feuds, vengeances etc. But when it came to issues of national interest, the Afghan rulers took the initiative and convened the Jirgas in order to get the nation involved in the affairs of the country.

G. Rauf Roashan, "Loya Jirga: One of the Last Political Tools for Bringing Peace to Afghanistan," www.institute-for-afghan-studies.org, February 13, 2005.

During the rest of the decade, Ahmad Shah conducted three further invasions into the Punjab to face his new Sikh opponents. This people, who practiced a combination of the Muslim and Hindu faiths, had emerged in the sixteenth century and after decades of persecution had hardened into excellent warriors. Twice, Ahmad Shah sacked their holy city, Amritsar, but each time the Sikhs closed in behind him when the Afghans returned to their mountains for the summer. On his final invasion, in 1769, Ahmad found that he was no longer able to assert control of the Punjab.

Toward an Afghan Nation

Ahmad Shah died in 1772 at age fifty after suffering from a horrible disease which might have been skin cancer. One visitor reported that late in his life he wore a silver nose, his original one having wasted away or perhaps been cut off in an attempt to stop the spread. By all accounts he was not only an excellent military leader but an admirable sovereign, who, while retaining his dignity, was solicitous of the concerns of his subjects. Like other pan-tribal leaders such as Attila and Genghis Khan, he was modest in his personal dress and habits while possessing an innate ability to draw the best efforts from others.

To many, his accession to the head of the Abdali tribe in 1747 marks the birth of the Afghan nation; others disagree because his creation was more of a Durrani empire than an Afghan state, indistinguishable from countless ephemeral tribal expansions that had come before. Both views have validity, and in Ahmad Shah, in fact, it is possible to see both a descendant of a Scythian nomad, leading his tribe on ever greater expeditions for plunder, and an Afghan who put his country before his tribe in a manner indistinguishable from modern patriotism. His own words, in a poem dedicated to his homeland, certainly reinforce the latter view:

> By blood, we are immersed in love of you.
> The youth lose their heads for your sake.
> I come to you and my heart finds rest.
> Away from you, grief clings to my heart like a snake.
> I forget the throne of Delhi
> When I remember the mountain tops of my Afghan land.
> If I must choose between the world and you,
> I shall not hesitate to claim your barren deserts as my own.

Although the Ghaznavids and Ghorids had established empires from within Afghanistan many centuries earlier, their ruling dynasties were Turkic rather than native. The Durrani achievement was to raise the Afghans themselves into a prominence that, in the Islamic world of the late eighteenth century, was matched only by the Ottomans. On balance it would seem that Ahmad Shah was not just a tribal chieftain but indeed the man who guided Afghanistan from its role as a boundary or no-man's-land between other empires into an independent political entity which, like Ahmad himself, deserved respect. His direct line would last as kings in Afghanistan until 1818, whereupon another branch of the Durranis would continue in office until the Communist coup of 1973. But while he established a royal precedent, it cannot be said that after the founder's death the kingdom continued on an upward trajectory.

The Decline of the Empire

Ahmad Shah's great failure was his inability to extend his own dynamism from beyond the grave, by providing an institutional means for his heirs to hold on to what he had won. This was the age-old problem of nomad tribal structures, which rose upon the will of dynamic leaders and collapsed just as rapidly when the strongman disappeared. Afghanistan, though having staked a claim to statehood, was still more a coalition of tribes, in a situation that toward the end of the eighteenth century was fast becoming an anachronism. Elsewhere in the world, tribal systems were being eradicated, absorbed, or colonized by more sophisticated nation-states. In the West, governmental institutions buoyed by literate populations were on the way to supplanting the prerogatives of kings. It should also be noted that the Durrani Empire was a Pashtun [Afghanistan's ethnic majority] effort rather than a multi-ethnic one; and even then, Ahmad Shah had found it necessary to bribe rather than persuade the Afridis [a tribe living in the Khyber Pass] and others to hold open the passes to India. On balance, though the modern boundaries of Afghanistan had yet to be established, Ahmad Shah had ensured that they soon would be, even in the face of the greatest empires of the modern era.

The Great Game: Great Britain and Russia Vie for Afghanistan

The Afghans Defeat the British Imperialists

By J. Talboys Wheeler and H. Le Poer Wynne

In the nineteenth century, Russia and Great Britain competed for control of Afghanistan. The Russians were expanding their empire south, seeking an outlet to the Indian Ocean. Threatened by Russian expansion, Great Britain wanted to protect its empire in India. This competition for Afghanistan became known as the Great Game. To reduce Russian influence in the area, British troops invaded Afghanistan in 1839, forcing out Afghan king Dost Mohammad Khan and installing Shah Shoja as a puppet leader in the capital of Kabul. The Afghan tribesmen resented this foreign imposition of Shah Shoja and began to rebel. In 1841 several hill tribes mounted an insurrection and began to besiege the British troops in Kabul.

The following selection is an account of the Anglo-Afghan War that ensued. Authors J. Talboys Wheeler and H. Le Poer Wynne describe how the Afghans revolted against the British in Kabul, killing British agents and capturing their garrison. The garrison surrendered in 1842, after which the Afghans agreed to offer a protective escort to the retreating British. However, the British were ambushed and massacred in the Khyber Pass by Afghan tribesmen. Of the forty-five hundred troops and the twelve thousand camp followers who fled from Kabul, only one man escaped to Jalalabad. Dost Mohammad Khan was restored to the throne in 1843.

J. Talboys Wheeler and H. Le Poer Wynne were members of the British Foreign Department and in 1869 prepared the report from which this selection is excerpted.

J. Talboys Wheeler and H. Le Poer Wynne, *The Political and Secret Files of the India Office*. London: L/P&s/20, 1869.

With [Afghan king] Dost [Mahomed Khan] out of the way Shah Shujah . . . suggested that he could maintain himself on the throne of Cabul without further assistance from Britain. Then, with suicidal rashness he reduced the subsidies paid to his army sirdars [persons of high rank]. Conspiracy soon followed, led by one Abdullah Khan. In October the Ghilzai tribesmen in the hills outside Cabul cut off all communications with the capital. Meanwhile, the British C-in-C [commander in chief] Sir John Keane was succeeded by Sir Willoughby Cotton and very soon after his place was taken by the aged and infirm General Elphinstone. On October 11, General Sale left Cabul with a brigade to open up again communication with Jelalabad. Every foot of territory was contested by the Ghilzais. For 18 days the force was slowly strangled in the hills. The tribesmen commanded the heights and were able to rain fire on the advancing columns. Sale's army was eventually able to take refuge at Jelalabad, while the force bringing up the rear nudged even closer to destruction. On 1 November 1841 there was a general rising of the hill tribes. Incredibly [Sir Alexander] Burnes and [Sir William] Macnaghten who were with the expedition both reported that all was quiet. 'The Afghan chiefs are sincerely attached to Shah Shujah', they reported. In Cabul itself the amorous adventures of British officers with the Afghan women were said to have excited jealousy and more anger. On November 2, 1841, being the day after the news of General Sale's struggle against the Ghilzais in the hills reached Cabul, insurrection broke out. Abdullah Khan, the head of the conspiracy, had ceased to conceal his intentions, and had openly threatened to slay Sir Alexander Burnes. All this had reached the ears of Burnes, but he treated it as sheer braggadocio; until he saw that the attitude assumed by Abdullah Khan was connected with the revolt in the hills. On the morning of November 2 he sent a servant to request Abdullah Khan to pay him a visit: but Abdullah Khan suspected that Burnes intended seizing him and sending him to India; and he therefore collected some of the conspirators, and proceeded with them to the house of Burnes, accompanied by a band of a hundred and thirty servants and followers. On their way they killed every British officer and soldier they met in the streets. Burnes heard of these massacres, and at first thought of escaping in disguise to the British cantonment, but he resolved to maintain the honour of the British name by remaining at his residence in British uniform. He then barricaded his house and sent messenger after messenger to Sir William Macnaghten to despatch a battalion of infantry and two pieces of artillery without delay. At that time such a force would have easily repressed the insurgents; for ten thousand Kuzzilbashes, Huzaras, and Parsivans [minor Afghan tribes] were prepared to rally round Burnes, but feared to take the initiative lest they should ultimately be punished by the Afghans. No force reached Burnes, yet the besieged, who only numbered thirty-three individuals, held out from eight o'clock in the morning till two in the afternoon, when the mob succeeded in burning down the great gate, and rushed in a mass through the passage. Burnes was killed on the spot and horribly mutilated. Twenty-three persons perished with him, and the remainder escaped by a miracle. The treasury of Captain Johnson, the Paymaster of Shah Shujah's army, was pillaged; and the guards at the pay office, like the escort at Burnes's house, were slaughtered almost to a man. The whole city was by this time in a tumult of excitement. Shops were quitted and houses were burned, and nothing was done to curb the disorder. The news of this plunder and riot rapidly attracted thousands of country people to the city, so that an insurrection that might have been put down by a small number of troops in the morning, could scarcely have been suppressed in the evening without the aid of a considerable army. Two days afterwards a fort containing the commissariat stores for the native army of Shah Shujah fell into the hands of the mob. Captain Colin Mackenzie, who was in charge, held out during these two days with notable courage; but meantime not a company arrived to relieve him, and after much trial and suffering his ammunition was exhausted and he was compelled to abandon the place and make his escape to the cantonment.

Burnes Is Besieged

All this while, six thousand British troops were in cantonments within half an hour's march of the city. The old Ameer [emir] Shah Shujah, who could hear the roar of the disturbances from the Bala Hissar (the royal citadel) although he could see but little of what was going on in the narrow winding streets below, sent out a Hindoostanee [Hindustani] regiment to put down the disorder; but this force lost itself in the maze of the city's streets, and accordingly abandoned their guns, and returned to the Bala Hissar.

Meantime there was culpable delay on the part of the British authorities in the cantonments. Sir William Macnaghten was told between seven and eight o'clock in the morning that Burnes's house was besieged, and he immediately communicated the news to General Elphinstone. It was then proposed to send Brigadier Shelton with two regiments and guns to the Bala Hissar; but General Elphinstone countermanded this order on the ground that Shah Shujah would object. (An inquiry acquitted Brigadier Shelton of all blame, and distributed the responsibility of the protracted delay between General Elphinstone and Sir William Macnaghten.) At first the outbreak was underrated. Then the advance of troops was deferred until Shah Shujah had been consulted. Then it was believed that Shah Shujah's regiment of Hindoostanees would put down the insurgents. Meantime the tide of insurrection had begun to flood the whole city. About midday Brigadier Shelton with a body of infantry and artillery moved into the Bala Hissar, but found that by this time it was impracticable to reach Burnes's house. Nothing further was done until three o'clock in the afternoon on the following day, when a weak force was sent under Major Swayne, but could not enter the city, and was compelled to return to cantonments. Sir W. Macnaghten had already removed his family from the residency into the cantonments, and on November 3, an attempt was made to improve the defences. From the very first, however, there had been a great deficiency in the artillery; and now as one battery had gone with General Sale's force to Jelalabad, and another had been sent to the Bala Hissar, only a miserable remnant remained in cantonments. On November 4, the commissariat fort, which contained all the stores for the British troops, fell into the hands of the enemy. It was situated about four hundred yards from the cantonment, and its communication was easily cut off, and the place itself exposed to fire from the rebels, until it was finally abandoned.

Zeman Khan Is Declared Ameer

On November 4, 1841, a wealthy Mohammadzai Sirdar named Zeman Khan, a nephew of Dost Mahomed Khan, succeeded by means of largesses in inducing the Afghans to proclaim him Ameer. This man made daily attacks upon the English cantonments. All this while Shah Shujah was in the Bala Hissar, and it was suggested that the British force should leave the cantonments without delay and take up a position in the Bala Hissar; as in such a position the British garrison could command the town, and compel the inhabitants to supply them with provisions. The plan, however, was rejected by General Elphinstone; and on November 9, Brigadier Shelton was recalled from the Bala Hissar, and returned to the cantonments. General Elphinstone was enfeebled with age and disease, and displayed a weakness and vacillation which created much discontent amongst the officers. There were also misunderstandings between General Elphinstone and Brigadier Shelton, which prevented their acting cordially together. At this juncture, Sir William Macnaghten despatched letters for the recall of General Sale's brigade, but Sale had already pushed on to Jelalabad, and no help was to be expected from that quarter.

An Entire Nation in Revolt

By now the whole country was in revolt against the British. The force at Ghuznee had been ordered to Cabul, but was unable to leave the citadel. A brigade had been recalled from Candahar, but was delayed by snow which had fallen and the rapid development of the insurrection; so that after throwing a garrison into Khelat-i-Ghilzai it was compelled to return to Candahar. Major Pottinger, who had arrived from Herat, reached Cabul wounded and alone. He brought the news that [the western town of] Chareekar was lost, that an entire Goorkha regiment had been annihilated, and that large bodies of Kohistanees and others had committed great atrocities in that quarter, and were proceeding to join the rebels at Cabul.

The first idea of Sir William Macnaghten, on hearing of these disasters, was to force a way to Jelalabad, which had been fortified by General Sale.

At this crisis, Mahomed Akbar Khan, the eldest son of Dost Mahomed Khan, appeared at Cabul. Some time previously, he had left Bokhara for Persia, but having heard of the insurrection, he turned back to Cabul, and reached the city on November 25. Here he found that Shah Shujah was shut up in the Bala Hissar, whilst his cousin, Zeman Khan, had been acknowledged Ameer. Mahomed Akbar Khan was vexed at seeing Zeman Khan in power, but thought it expedient to recognise his election to the throne. He then endeavoured to create a party for himself, and now began to exercise an important influence upon the progress of affairs.

All hope of being reinforced from Jelalabad or Candahar had now died out; and the demoralisation of the army, and utter failure of supplies, literally forced Sir William Macnaghten to commence negotiations. On December 11 a conference ensued on the bank of the Cabul river. On one side were Sir William Macnaghten and Captains Lawrence, Trevor and Mackenzie; on the other were Mahomed Akbar Khan and other leading chiefs of Afghanistan. A draft treaty was submitted by Sir William Macnaghten, and after much discussion, the main stipulations were agreed upon. It was admitted that recent events had proved that the presence of a British army at Afghanistan for the support of Shah Shujah was displeasing to the great majority of the Afghan nation; and that as the British government had sent its troops into Afghanistan with the sole object of promoting the welfare of the people, so it was prepared to withdraw them when the army ceased to accomplish the end desired. It was thereupon agreed that the British troops at Cabul should return at once to Peshawar, and thence to India; that the force at Jelalabad should retire as soon as Sir William Macnaghten was satisfied that the progress of the Cabul army would not be interrupted; and that the forces at Ghuznee and Candahar should follow their example, as soon as arrangements could be made. The Afghan Sirdars agreed to assist the British forces with carriage and provisions, and to leave them unmolested. Shah Shujah was to be allowed to accompany the British army on its return to India, or to remain in Afghanistan on a stipend of not less than one lakh of rupees per annum. Immediately on the safe arrival of the British troops at Peshawar, arrangements were to be made for the return of Dost Mahomed Khan, and all other Afghans who had been detained in India. Four British officers would be left at Cabul as hostages for the safe return of Dost Mahomed Khan and his family; and Mahomed Akbar Khan, and such other Sirdars of influence as pleased, were to accompany the British troops to Peshawar. It was also agreed that the British force would evacuate its cantonments within three days, and that meanwhile the Afghan Sirdars should send in provisions for their use.

Retreat Delayed

Preparations were now made for the immediate retreat of the British army; but a variety of circumstances prevented its departure. Fresh conferences arose as regarded the disposal of Shah Shujah. The promised carriage and supplies were withheld, and when furnished were intercepted by robbers and fanatics. On December 13 the small force still remaining in the Bala Hissar managed to return to the cantonments, but were much harassed by the Ghilzais. On December 18 snow began to fall, and at sunset was inches thick on the ground. The departure was then fixed for the 22nd. On the 19th Sir William Macnaghten and General Elphinstone despatched letters to Ghuznee, Candahar and Jelalabad, ordering the British forces to leave those positions. Meantime the Afghan Sirdars increased their demands. They called on the British authorities to deliver up all their military stores and ammunition, and to surrender the married families as hostages for the fulfilment of the treaty. All this while Sir William Macnaghten was vainly attempting to deliver the British force from the perils by which it was surrounded. On one hand he was in treaty with the Barukzai Sirdars; but he is also said to have offered large sums to the Ghilzais and Kuzzilbashes to take part with the English.

On December 2, Mahomed Akbar Khan sent new proposals of his own to Sir William Macnaghten. It was suggested that the British army should remain at Cabul until the spring, and should then withdraw as if of its own free will; and that Shah Shujah should continue to reign as Ameer with Mahomed Akbar Khan as his Vizier; whilst Mahomed Akbar Khan was to receive an annuity of four lakhs of rupees from the British government, and a bonus of thirty lakhs. Sir William Macnaghten accepted the proposal, and on December 23, he set out with the three officers of his staff, Captains Lawrence, Trevor and Mackenzie, to meet Mahomed Akbar Khan at a spot about six hundred yards from the cantonments. Mahomed Akbar Khan arrived soon afterwards accompanied by several Sirdars. After an exchange of salutations, the English officers seated themselves with the Sirdars, and meantime crowds of armed Afghans clustered around. Mahomed Akbar Khan abruptly opened the proceedings by asking the envoy if he were ready to carry out the arrangements proposed. Sir William Macnaghten replied in the affirmative. At that moment Sir William Macnaghten and his three companions were violently seized from behind. The three companions were each compelled to mount a horse which was ridden by an Afghan Sirdar, and were soon running the gauntlet through a crowd of religious fanatics known as Ghazees, who struck at them as they passed. Captain Trevor slipped from his seat, and was cut to pieces. Captains Lawrence and Mackenzie fortunately escaped with their lives although still prisoners. Meantime Sir William Macnaghten was struggling desperately on the ground with Mahomed Akbar Khan; and at length Mahomed Akbar Khan, who only desired to take him prisoner, drew his pistol and shot him through the head. The infuriated Ghazees then hacked his body to pieces with their knives.

Treaty Negotiations

Although this bloody atrocity was committed within so short a distance, General Elphinstone refused to believe that the envoy had been murdered. He even sent his adjutant, Captain Grant, to assure the British troops that the conference had been interrupted by the Ghazees and that Sir William Macnaghten and his companions had been removed to the city, but would return immediately to cantonments. At this very time, the mangled remains of the British envoy were being triumphantly paraded through the streets and bazaars of the city.

Overtures for negotiations were renewed by the Afghan chiefs through Captain Lawrence. Major Pottinger had been incapacitated by his wounds since his return from Chareekar; but the garrison turned to him as the only man fitted to succeed to the vacant post of envoy. Pottinger insisted the army should attempt either to occupy the Bala Hissar until spring, or to fight its way to Jelalabad. The military authorities, however, urged that there was no other course but negotiations; and on January 1, 1842, the treaty which had been previously drawn up by Sir William Macnaghten was ratified by Major Pottinger and the Afghan Sirdars.

On January 6, 1842, the British force left the cantonments under General England, after a humiliation which had lasted for sixty-five days. Scarcely had the cantonments been vacated, when the Afghans rushed in and set every building on fire, and destroyed everything which they could not carry away. The Afghan parties to the treaty, who had agreed to furnish an escort to protect the force from the Ghazees and bandits, failed to keep to their bargain. A great mass of camp followers accompanied the army, and were exposed to incessant attacks by fanatics and robbers. Yet the retreating party laboured on through the snow. The next day, January 7, discipline was rapidly disappearing, and the army was becoming a rabble. Mahomed Akbar Khan made his appearance with six hundred horsemen, and reproached the

British authorities for their hasty retreat on the previous day. He said that he had come to protect them from the Ghazees; but he demanded more hostages as security for the evacuation of Jelalabad. He also announced that he would supply the force with everything they required, but would arrest its progress until General Sale had retired from Jelalabad. The same evening the force encamped at Bootkhak, at the entrance of the Khoord Cabul Pass [also known as the Khyber Pass]. Major Pottinger, Captain Lawrence, and Captain Colin Mackenzie then remained as hostages with Mahomed Akbar Khan; and it was agreed that the force should push on from Bootkhak through the Pass of Khoord Cabul to Tezeen, and halt at Tezeen until the arrival of the news that General Sale had withdrawn from Jelalabad.

Deadly Retreat

For five miles the Pass of Khoord Cabul runs between precipitous mountain ranges, and here it seemed that Mahomed Akbar Khan was wholly unable to defend the retreating party from the enemy. The heights were crowned by hordes of fanatic Ghilzais, who poured a deadly fire on the struggling rabble. Public and private baggage of every description was now abandoned by the fugitives; and three thousand men are said to have perished from gun fire, or to have dropped down exhausted to be dispatched by the knives of the Afghans.

The next morning, January 9, Mahomed Akbar Khan induced General Elphinstone to countermand the order to march, by offering to supply provisions, and engaging to do his best for the future protection of the retreating body. Mahomed Akbar Khan now proposed that all the ladies and children should be placed in his charge to be conducted in safety to Peshawar; and accordingly the widows, wives and children became the 'guests' of Mahomed Akbar Khan, and the married officers went with them.

On January 10, the remnant of the force, which had been weakened by desertion as well as by death, resumed its march. The savage Ghilzais renewed their murderous attacks. The troops were frostbitten, paralyzed, and panic-stricken. Mahomed Akbar Khan, attended by his horsemen, watched the butchery that was going on below, but again declared himself utterly unable to restrain the Ghilzais. Throughout the night and the next day, the remnant struggled on beneath the deadly fire of the Ghilzais to Jugdulluk, and there halted behind some ruined walls. Here Mahomed Akbar Khan appeared and invited General Elphinstone, Brigadier Shelton, and Captain Johnson to another conference. Food and tea were placed before the three English officers, and they were kindly entertained; but Mahomed Akbar Khan insisted upon retaining them as hostages for the evacuation of Jelalabad. Again he promised to restrain the tribes from attacking the remnant of the force during the rest of the march; but meantime the petty chiefs of the country between Jugdulluk and Jelalabad came flocking in, and utterly refused to give a safe conduct to the few remaining troops to Jelalabad. At last two lakhs of rupees were offered and accepted. On the 12th the remnant of the army pushed on to the Jugdulluk Pass, but found the mouth of the Pass blocked up by a barricade. A terrible massacre ensued which resulted in the literal destruction of the force. A few individuals only escaped, and they were as one to a hundred. They reached Gundamuck, but were there attacked by a mob which cut them down almost to a man. Thus perished a force which left Cabul with four thousand five hundred fighting men and twelve thousand camp followers. One man only escaped to Jelalabad, and this was Dr Brydon. The garrison saw him from the walls, wounded, famished, and travel-worn, clinging to a wretched pony. He was brought in half dead, and announced his belief that he was the only survivor of the sixteen thousand men.

Meantime, Dost Mahomed Khan, who had been residing under surveillance at Calcutta, had been escorted to Shikarpore and formally set at liberty. He at once determined on returning to Afghanistan, but proceeded in the first instance to Lahore, where he was splendidly entertained by Shere Singh, who was now Maharaja [ruler] of the Punjab. Here Dost Mahomed Khan received intelligence of the progress of affairs in Afghanistan. It seems that the British army had scarcely crossed the Indus, when Mahomed Akbar Khan reappeared at Cabul, and attacked and dethroned Shapoor Mirza, a younger son of Shah Shujah, who had endeavoured to establish himself in the supreme authority. At the same time, however, the party of Zeman Khan was reconstituted and arrayed against Mahomed Akbar Khan; and the latter was compelled to retire into the Bala Hissar, and was besieged there for ten weeks. On receipt of these tidings Dost Mahomed Khan sent his four sons with all haste to Cabul, namely, Mahomed Afzul Khan, Mahomed Akrum Khan, Mahomed Azim Khan, and Gholam Hyder Khan. The young men arrived at Cabul only just in time to relieve their beleaguered brother. Dost Mahomed Khan followed shortly afterwards, and was received by the people, after a banishment of three years, as the Ameer of Cabul.

About the same time Kohandil Khan, the brother of Dost Mahomed Khan, and ex-ruler of Candahar, returned from Persia, where he had been residing since his flight in 1839, and became once again independent ruler of Candahar.

Afghanistan Becomes a Buffer State

By Abdul Samad Ghaus

Throughout the nineteenth century Afghanistan was threatened by the two imperialistic nations of Russia and Great Britain as each tried to expand its holdings in central Asia. However, in 1873 Russia and Great Britain signed the Russo-British Agreement on Afghanistan. According to the agreement, Russia recognized that Afghanistan belonged to the British sphere of influence. In return, the British accepted Russia's annexation of land to the north of Afghanistan, thereby establishing Afghanistan's northern border. Afghanistan thus became a buffer state between the British and Russian empires. In 1893 Great Britain pressured Afghanistan to agree to a southern border that became known as the Durand Line, after Mortimer Durand, the British diplomat who forced the agreement on Afghan leader Abdul Rhaman Khan. The two border agreements cost Afghanistan a significant amount of territory and divided tribal lands in a way that led to conflict that continues today. In the following selection Abdul Samad Ghaus describes the development of Afghanistan as a buffer state and the detrimental consequences of the border agreements for the nation. Ghaus is a former deputy foreign minister of Afghanistan and has represented the country in the United Nations.

The possession of India has always held a strange fascination for the great Asian and European empire builders. To those conquerors who succeeded in incorporating India or parts of it into their dominions, the securing of these lands against other foreign intruders became a prime consideration, almost an end in itself. Of the alien occupiers of India, perhaps none was more sensitive to this outside threat than the British.

Abdul Samad Ghaus, *The Fall of Afghanistan: An Insider's Account*. Washington, DC: Pergamon-Brassey's International Defense Publishers, 1988. Copyright © 1988 by Pergamon-Brassey's International Defense Publishers, Inc. All rights reserved. Reproduced by permission of Potomac Books, Inc.

As British rule in the nineteenth century expanded into north-western India, its defense increasingly occupied the minds of the British rulers. In fact, their concern for the defense of India began to determine the formulation of their eastern policies, if not their foreign policy altogether. British sensitivity in this regard grew rapidly with the emergence of czarist Russia as a dynamic imperial power in central Asia and its seemingly inexorable southward move.

By the mid–nineteenth century Russia's threat to the subcontinent and its desire to reach the warm waters of the Indian Ocean were generally accepted as realities in Britain and India. With the exception of short intervals during World War I and World War II, this British perception of czarist danger to India and later of the Soviet menace to that country remained constant until 1947, when Britain's rule in India came to an abrupt end.

Thus, as soon as the two European empires, Russia and Britain, began facing each other in central Asia, although still from a respectable distance, fear of a Russian advance into India prompted the British rulers to turn their most serious attention to the regions that lay between the areas that Britain had reached in northern India and the shifting frontiers of the czarist empire. In fact [according to scholar W.K. Fraser-Tytler] the British realized, as the previous rulers of India had known, that "the safety of India depends on the degree of control which the rulers of India can exert on the mountains of Hindu Kush and the Oxus Valley beyond, for only thus can the 'barbarian' be kept at arm's length."

On the basis of this consideration, the British sought to maintain outposts and adequate influence in the peripheral regions, with a view to monitoring Russia's movements and eventually forestalling its advance. These preoccupations led the British to interfere openly in the internal affairs of the states and principalities situated between Russia and them, often to the detriment of those areas' independence. Afghanistan, which lay directly in the path of an eventual Russian advance from the northwest and whose strategic significance in relation to the Russian Asian empire was becoming increasingly clear, came to be particularly affected by these British preoccupations. The British interfered extensively in the internal affairs of Afghanistan and twice during the nineteenth century occupied it militarily.

The British push toward Afghanistan and occupation of advanced positions there came to be called *forward policy*. This policy was at times discontinued in favor of a more restrained *masterly inactivity*, but it was clear that the latter attitude merely meant the forswearance of *military* intervention and occupation and not the total cessation of *political* interference. Then, for the sake of the defense of India, a time came when the British were ready to test the merits of a third formula: the establishment of Afghanistan as a buffer state between the Russian empire and India. . . .

Russia Advances

Meanwhile, Russia's advance into central Asia was continuing unabated. The British sought an explanation on several occasions from the czarist government as to where it finally intended to stop. Prince Gorchakov, the imperial Russian chancellor, issued a memorandum in 1864 in which he explained the motives for the Russian advance and assured the other powers that the line reached at that time was considered by the czarist government to be the outer limits of the empire. Gorchakov's memorandum was a typical nineteenth-century imperial document, attempting to convey the impression that the whole of central Asia was populated by half-savage tribes and that Russian territorial expansion was only accidental, its main purposes being the security of the people inside the Russian frontiers and the propagation of Western civilization.

However, whether the Asians were willing to accept Western civilization in return for their freedom was not discussed in the memorandum. According to the Russian rationalization, the wandering Asiatic tribes would start raiding and pillaging the people inside Russian territory. This state of affairs would compel the government to punish them and, for the sake of security, to annex their territory. After a while, the newly acquired territory would become exposed to the aggression of more distant tribes. The state would be obliged once again to defend the population by mounting a new expedition and punishing those who committed aggression. Thus the cycle of punishment and annexation continued and so did the expansion of Russian territory. It was evident that Gorchakov, by circulating his memorandum, was asking for understanding and even appreciation of Russian expansionist policies in Asia. The greatest difficulty, according to the memorandum, was "in knowing when to stop." The memorandum went on to announce that the actual line reached, just short of the community of Khokand, was the limit of Russian expansion in Asia. However, the ink on Gorchakov's memorandum had hardly dried when the Russians invaded Khokand and occupied it.

Thus, the Gorchakov memorandum lacked any validity. One author has written that this extraordinary document either was a masterpiece of deception or St. Petersburg [former capital of Russia] was totally unable to control its commanders on the frontiers. The British government renewed its efforts to extract from the Russians some formal assurances as to their ultimate goal. At the same time, the British attempted to induce the Russians to accept the maintenance of a "neutral zone" or "belt of independent states" between the two empires in Asia as a means of preserving them from potentially antagonistic contact.

Buffer Zone

This idea of a neutral zone or belt of independent states, precursor of the buffer arrangements of later years, had been occasionally aired by prominent British statesmen. In 1869, the British foreign secretary recommended to the Russian ambassador in London "the recognition of some territory as neutral between the possessions of England and Russia." Lord Mayo, the viceroy of India, suggested in 1870 that

> [A]s it is for the interests of both countries that a wide border of independent states should exist between the British frontier and the Russian boundary, it would be desirable that Russia should be invited to adopt the policy with regard to Khiva and other kindred States (Bokhara and Khokand) that we are willing to pledge ourselves to adopt towards Kalat, Afghanistan and the districts around Yarkent. A pledge of mutual non-interference of this kind, unratified by treaty, would be alike honourable to both nations, and would be better suited to the position in which civilized powers must ever stand towards wild and savage tribes than any specific treaty engagements could ever be.

As the British probing of St. Petersburg's intentions continued, it became apparent that, in a settlement, the czarist government wanted the rich northern plains of Afghanistan, including the region of Badakhshan, to be included in its domains. If that were not feasible, the Russians felt it should be recognized that they had the right to extend their control at least to the ill-defined northern Afghan border. The British realized that, sooner or later, the inclusion of the trans-Oxus lands in the czarist empire would become a fait accompli. That being Russia's goal, it obviously could not be expected to accept the establishment of a neutral zone or belt of independent states that would extend beyond the northern borders of Afghanistan. The British therefore understood that their most urgent task in their dealings with the Russians was to obtain at least the maintenance of Afghanistan's integrity, even if that meant Russian occupation of the whole area north of the Oxus.

This trend in British thinking created a favorable impression in St. Petersburg. As the subject of a proposed neutral zone or belt of independent states (which, in the British view included, besides Afghanistan, some of the trans-Oxus lands) dropped from Russo-British exchanges, the Russian government agreed that Afghanistan was outside its sphere of influence and that it could constitute a distinct entity between the two empires. By adhering to that position, moreover, the Russians implicitly conceded that the northern border of Afghanistan would be the limit of their territorial expansion in central Asia. That position freed the Russians from any scruples they might have entertained concerning the extension of their dominion to the banks of the Oxus.

Russia and Great Britain Agree on Afghanistan

After protracted negotiations and the exchange of voluminous correspondence, the two powers signed the Russo-British Agreement on Afghanistan in 1873. This was the first major agreement between the two powers concerning Afghanistan, and it came to be known as the Clarendon-Gorchakov Agreement. In it Russia accepted the exclusion of Afghanistan from its zone of influence and recognized a frontier between Afghanistan and its own future annexations in central Asia. British Prime Minister Gladstone had this to say in the House of Commons about the 1873 agreement: "The engagement referred solely to the moral influence possessed by England and Russia in the East; Russia engaging to abstain from an attempt to exercise it in Afghanistan and England engaging to exercise it for a pacific purpose." In fact, a bargain had been struck. In return for British acquiescence to Russian subjugation of the lands beyond Afghanistan's northern border, the Russians recognized that country as falling outside their sphere of influence and within that of the British. . . .

The 1873 agreement had strengthened the idea of transforming Afghanistan into a buffer state in central Asia between the British and Russian empires. When Britain evacuated Afghanistan in 1880 and entrusted its destinies to the new monarch, Amir Abdul Rahman Khan, that concept, as the British understood it, was ready for implementation.

The buffer formula, which, for all practical purposes, did not preclude control of Afghan affairs by the British, was a middle course between military occupation of Afghanistan and stoically waiting for Russian armies to enter the subcontinent. It also implied that the British northwestern push had, for a variety of reasons, finally come to an end and that Britain was now interested solely in defending its Indian possessions behind the shield of a buffer state. This implication of the buffer concept was one of its significant drawbacks. It was bound to convey a sense of retreat, and retreat for a first-class power could not be devoid of danger. But the British hoped that a combination of various elements, of which the assertive role of the Afghan ruler was not the least important, would preserve the viability of the buffer state and consequently the security of India.

The Russian Arkhal expedition had stopped short of the oasis of Merv, its logical objective in that expansionary episode, when the Russians learned that the British were evacuating the whole of Afghanistan. However, three years later, in 1884, Russia annexed Merv, despite all previous assurances to the contrary. At the time this event occurred, British forces had long since left Afghanistan, and there existed no direct British threat to Russia's central Asian possessions.

The British, to say the least, were uneasy about Russia's conquest of Merv, which they considered a threat to Herat, little more than two hundred flat and easily traversable miles to the south. Judging the Russians by their past performance, the British government believed that Russia would not stop at Merv and would sooner or later invade Herat. It was therefore essential to forestall Russia's further advance. The British government, basing its position on the relevant provisions of the 1873 agreement between Russia and Britain concerning the northern frontier of Afghanistan, wanted Russia to formally recognize a demarcated northern Afghan frontier, the western part of which was to constitute a clearly defined line between Herat and Merv. After months of stalling, the Russians agreed to negotiate.

More Negotiations

While negotiations were underway in London and in St. Petersburg, the czarist empire once again moved southward. In March of 1885, Russia seized Panjdeh, an integral part of Afghanistan. Panjdeh was a district of Badghis, which in turn was part of the province of Herat. The Russian aim in capturing Panjdeh was quite clear. In doing so they were laying the groundwork for a move on Herat. They were also testing British determination, to ascertain whether Britain would categorically deny them any further territorial acquisitions in the region.

While an enthusiastic Russian press was exhorting the government not to stop and to push on to Herat, the British government and people reacted with a rare intensity to the fall of Panjdeh. Two army corps were mobilized in India. The House of Commons was asked to vote substantial war credits. British army engineers were dispatched to Herat to assist the Afghans in fortifying the city.

Taking stock of the seriousness of British preparations, the Russian government realized that Britain was determined not to allow it any further encroachment on Afghan territory and that another advance toward Herat would certainly mean war between the two empires. That unambiguous British attitude, and perhaps the rise of Germany in Europe as a formidable rival to both the czarist empire and Britain, prompted the Russians to adopt a conciliatory position. Russia halted its southward advance, waiting for more favorable times and conditions to resume it.

Boundary negotiations were reactivated. The line of the Russo-Afghan frontier, beginning at Zulfiquar in the west, running eastward between Merv and the province of Herat to the Oxus, and following that river to Lake Victoria and the Chinese frontier in the northeast, was formally agreed upon and demarcated in stages. The Russians retained Panjdeh in the process. During the protracted negotiations between Britain and Russia that led to the Frontier Agreement, the amir of Afghanistan was never more than a distant observer. In the end he had to accept what had been agreed upon in his absence.

When the northern border of Afghanistan was formally agreed upon in 1895, in the view of the British, two of the most important elements of a viable buffer state were at last in place. First, Amir Abdul Rahman Khan, a strong monarch whose foreign policy remained firmly under British control and who in all likelihood would prevent the spread of Russian influence, had been installed in Afghanistan. Second, the buffer state's formally recognized northern border, the violation of which would constitute a breach of international law, had become a reality. . . .

The evolution of Afghanistan as a buffer between Russia and India had a long and tenuous process. But in the early 1880s the British could look at the results with some satisfaction: the Indian empire seemed secure behind the formidable barrier of the buffer, a fluid situation had been stabilized, and, in all likelihood, the "Great Game" [the competition between Russia and Great Britain] in central Asia had finally come to an end. So far as Afghanistan was concerned, with the acquisition of the status of a buffer, it slipped slowly into oblivion.

What Afghanistan Lost

As a British protectorate, Afghanistan was kept economically weak and politically isolated. On various occasions the British professed that they wanted Afghanistan to be strong and independent. But a strong and independent Afghanistan meant one thing to them and quite another to the Afghan rulers and people. The Afghan rulers, during the heydey of British colonialism, were constantly reminded that their existence depended on the will and the tolerance of the British and that the fate of their country could even be decided in concert by London and St. Petersburg without consulting them. Consequently, the Afghan kings were so preoccupied with the preservation of their throne and Afghanistan's territorial integrity that not enough time, money, or energy could be devoted to development of the country.

While the British determination to keep foreign intruders away from India may have saved Afghanistan from being absorbed by the Russians in the nineteenth century, the defense of India nevertheless left deep and long-lasting scars on Afghanistan and its people. The two Anglo-Afghan wars [the wars between Great Britain and Russia that took place from 1839 to 1842 and from 1878 to 1880], in addition to causing substantial loss of life and property, brought to the surface xenophobic sentiments that lingered for many years and proved powerful deterrents to Western-style reforms and innovations undertaken by Afghan rulers decades later. The high-handed and aggressive attitude of the British had convinced the population that they would not rest until Afghanistan, the last independent Islamic country of central Asia, was wiped off the map. This state of mind created resentment of the British, of Europeans, and of everything foreign.

Further, as a result of British and Russian incursions, Afghanistan lost territory to Russia in the north and to Britain in the east and southeast. In addition to the eastern Pashtun lands (which, in the not so distant past, had belonged to Afghanistan and whose inhabitants ethnically, religiously, and culturally were the same as Afghanistan's Pashtuns), Khyber, Kurram, Pishin, and Sibi were also incorporated into British India, and the so-called tribal area was erected as a buffer between India and Afghanistan. The Afghan claim to the eastern Pashtun lands was never taken seriously by the British. Despite Britain's reputation for having great knowledge of the East and its people, it never understood the reality and the depth of Afghan sentiment on this issue. By not attempting to settle the problem, which was an outgrowth of policies related to the defense of India, the British, perhaps inadvertently, sowed the seeds of discord between Afghanistan and the future state of Pakistan. The friction between the two countries brought about by the lingering existence of that colonial legacy helped pave the way for future Russian inroads into Afghanistan.

Afghanistan's Mechanics of Survival

Amir Abdul Rahman Khan fully understood the precarious geographical situation of his country. The amir and his court generally believed that the policies of czarist Russia were offensive and aimed at the ultimate conquest of India and, thus, naturally, the occupation and destruction of Afghanistan. Because of this belief, the amir may have "feared Russia more than Great Britain, for he saw that the Russian advance was one of accretion and incorporation—in the manner of an elephant, as he put it, 'who examines a spot thoroughly before he places his foot down upon it, and when he once places his foot there, there is no going back'" [as historian Arnold Fletcher notes].

Some influential members of the court were of the opinion that British northwestern expansion had run its course and that, consequently, the English rulers did not feel any compulsion to annex parts of Afghanistan. This passive British posture, however, did not mean that the Afghans, including the amir, felt assured that Britain would never again violate Afghanistan's national territory. Past history bore testimony to the fact that, whenever the British felt a resumption of forward policy would best address a particular threat to India, considerations about the preservation of Afghanistan's territorial integrity never deterred them from moving into that country.

Afghanistan's geopolitical situation necessarily determined the Afghan ruler's foreign policy. His policy could be nothing other than the preservation of an independent Afghanistan as a buffer between the two rival empires. "Abdul Rahman knew that the powers that agreed to a buffer between their territories could also agree to divide the country; the existence of an independent buffer was desirable at that time, but not vital to his neighbors [according to historian Ludwig W. Adamec]."

To ensure the survival of Afghanistan as an independent entity, the amir embarked on a foreign policy aimed at keeping a certain balance between his two mighty neighbors. The cardinal requisite for the maintenance of that equilibrium was, in the amir's view, adherence to strict isolationism, in order to keep British and Russian influence out of the country. The British were to be convinced that they could count on Afghan friendship and that Afghanistan and India were complementary in the defense of India against Russia, the common enemy. They were to be made aware that Britain's too close ties with Afghanistan and its greater influence in that country would render Russia suspicious and might provoke it into aggression. On the other hand, the Russians were to be given no reason to doubt the amir's determination to preserve Afghanistan as an independent entity. They were to be given no opportunity to believe that Afghanistan would willingly open its territory to an invasion of Russian central Asia by Britain.

As a corollary to this policy of balance, it was important for the amir to demonstrate that the buffer was stable and indivisible and that its stability served to maintain peace and tranquility on the borders of Russia and India. Certainly one of the aims of the amir's internal consolidation of power was to achieve the kind of stability that would render the perpetuation of the buffer attractive to its neighbors. Undoubtedly the stability of Abdul Rahman Khan's Afghanistan contributed to the realization that the buffer was useful and to the advantage of the two empires. . . .

The Fate of the Frontier

As time passed, relations between the amir and the British grew
more strained. The major issue between them was, of course, the
fate of the Frontier, or the eastern Pashtuns, whom the amir considered part of the Afghan nation. The amir felt that he was free
to have open intercourse with them, and most of the eastern
Pashtuns considered him, if not their sovereign, at least their spiritual leader. He provided them with guns and money, and, in return, they almost always heeded his call for jihad (holy war). Like
all other Afghan rulers, Abdul Rahman Khan considered the
Pashtun tribes one of the bulwarks of Afghanistan. He often used
the tribes to pressure the British or to relieve pressure from them.
In so doing he also indirectly demonstrated to the Russians the
leverage that he could use in his dealings with Britain and his ascendancy in that sensitive region. Britain wanted the amir to desist from aiding and abetting the tribes in their anti-British activities and to recognize British sovereignty in the tribal areas. But,
to their great disenchantment, the amir, while paying lip service
to the British, never changed his basic attitude with respect to the
Pashtun tribes.

A break in relations between Afghanistan and Britain seemed
imminent in the second half of 1883, when Abdul Rahman
Khan was asked by the government of India to receive a British
representative empowered to conduct negotiations with a view
to delimiting the frontier between Afghanistan and India. For
some time, the British had been steadily escalating their military
operations against the independent tribes in order to extend their
influence over them. Meanwhile, resistance by the tribes was becoming increasingly effective. The British suspected that the amir
had a hand in the concerted tribal response to their new forward
policy. British Viceroy Lord Lansdowne, a proponent of the forward policy on the Frontier, was of the opinion that a majority
of the problems related to disturbances in the tribal area could
be solved by delimiting the frontier. In his view, the delimitation
would, first, solve the issue of disputed territories and, second,
enable the British more easily to disarm and control the tribes
under their jurisdiction. Third, it would make it difficult for
Afghan agents and weapons to reach the eastern Pashtuns.

Amir Abdul Rahman Khan refused to receive the British representative to discuss delimitation of the frontier. Lord Lansdowne
reacted by ordering an embargo on all shipments of arms and

metal to Afghanistan and, when the amir still did not change his mind, threatened him with military intervention. Thereupon, war preparations started in India. The amir, knowing full well how his country had suffered in the past from the consequences of British forward policy, adopted a more conciliatory attitude. He informed the government of India that it could send its representative.

The Durand Line

In September 1893, Sir Mortimer Durand, the government of India's foreign secretary, arrived in Kabul carrying with him concrete British demands for a well-defined buffer zone between Afghanistan and India. The amir was horrified when he became acquainted with the nature and extent of those demands, according to which territories and people who since time immemorial had been considered part of the Afghan homeland and nation were arbitrarily included in British India. Some of the tribes and their lands were dissected, one part remaining attached to Afghanistan and the other given to India. Durand was not prepared to entertain the amir's objections, since the government of India had already decided upon the line that the frontier would follow. The amir soon realized that he was defending a lost cause and that, in fact, he had been confronted with an ultimatum. Disgusted with the heavy-handed, imperialistic handling of the matter by the government of India, he reluctantly agreed to the frontier as set by the British. Only two small districts that were to be given to India in the original British proposals were, in the end, given to Afghanistan.

On November 12, 1893, Abdul Rahman Khan signed, under duress, the frontier agreement known as the Durand Agreement. Thus, by British diktat, one nation and one land were cut in two, separated by an artificial frontier, the notorious Durand Line. The most disastrous effect of the agreement for the Afghans was that, by accepting it, the amir had in fact officially sanctioned British annexation of the lands east and south of the line, lands originally belonging to Afghanistan.

Afghanistan Achieves Independence

By David Fromkin

In 1907 Russia and Great Britain signed the Anglo-Russian Convention, which set forth their rights and obligations in Afghanistan. Great Britain promised to prevent Afghanistan from encroaching on Russian territory and was given the right to control Afghanistan's political affairs as long as it did not attempt to force a change of regime. Afghanistan became an official neutral zone, yet conflict did not end. Russia nibbled at Afghanistan's northern borders, and the British installed a puppet king and dictated the country's foreign policy, causing wide resentment among Afghans who found themselves living in a British colony in all but name.

In 1919 anti-British forces within Afghanistan assassinated the puppet leader, Emir Habibullah Khan. His son Amanullah took over, determined to gain his country's independence. Amanullah sent troops through the Khyber Pass to invade India. The result was the Third Anglo-Afghan War, described in the following excerpt by David Fromkin. Fromkin notes that even though the British were able to expel the Afghan troops from India, they realized they could not successfully invade and occupy Afghanistan. The British therefore relinquished control over the country's foreign affairs, and Afghanistan became independent. David Fromkin is a professor of history and international relations at Boston University. He has written essays and several books on history and politics, including A Peace to End All Peace.

E gypt, with its vital Suez Canal, was one of the key strategic positions on Britain's road to India. Afghanistan, with its mountain passes leading into the Indian plains, was another. Over the course of a century British armies had repeatedly been bloodied in the course of their efforts to prevent hos-

David Fromkin, *A Peace to End All Peace: The Fall of the Ottoman Empire and the Creation of the Modern Middle East.* New York: Henry Holt and Company, 1989. Copyright © 1989 by David Fromkin. Reproduced by permission of Henry Holt and Company LLC.

tile forces from controlling the fierce mountain kingdom. The issue was believed by British statesmen to have been resolved satisfactorily in 1907, when Russia agreed that the kingdom should become a British protectorate.

On 19 February 1919, however, the Emir of Afghanistan [Habibullah Khan] was assassinated; and after a short period in which rival claimants maneuvered for the succession, his third son, 26-year-old Amanullah Khan, wrote to the Governor-General of India announcing his accession to the "free and independent Government of Afghanistan." By the terms of Britain's agreement with Russia in 1907, Afghanistan was not, of course, fully free and independent, for Britain was entrusted with the conduct of her foreign relations. Yet on 19 April the new ruler went on to assert his complete independence in external as well as internal affairs.

Secret Plan

Amanullah secretly planned an attack on British India—through the Khyber Pass—that was to coincide with an Indian nationalist uprising in Peshawar, the principal British garrison town near the frontier. Amanullah believed that a nationwide Indian uprising would then occur.

Amanullah's army commander moved too soon, however, before the Peshawar uprising could be organized, and unwittingly alerted the British to their danger. On 3 May 1919 a detachment of Afghan troops crossed the frontier into British India at the top of the Khyber Pass. They seized control of a border village and a pumping station controlling the water supply to a nearby Indian military post. On 5 May the Governor-General of India telegraphed to London that it looked as though a war—the Third Afghan War—had started.

According to Amanullah, he had ordered his troops to the frontier in response to the British repression of disturbances in India. Referring to the Amritsar Massacre[1] and to the policy for which it stood, Amanullah declared that in the name of Islam and of humanity, he regarded the peoples of India as justified in rising up against British rule, and that his own troops were at the frontier to keep disorder from spreading.

1. On April 11, 1919, a small British military force in the Indian city of Amritsar, the holy city of the Sikhs, opened fire on a group of people who had assembled in a public park for a political meeting, killing 379 of them.

The British were unsure of his intentions. They were aware that during the war [World War I] a German military mission had nearly persuaded the Afghan government to launch an invasion of India, and they believed that Enver's old pan-Turkish colleagues, and also the new Bolshevik government in Russia, might influence the Afghan government in dangerous ways. Alarming information reaching the British authorities in May, at the time Amanullah's troops crossed the border, indicated that the Afghans planned a simultaneous attack on three fronts, spearheaded by hordes of religious fanatics, responding to the proclamation of a Holy War, and supported by regular troops in coordination with frontier tribes; while, at the same time, British forces were to be immobilized by mass rioting within India.

Believing that prompt action was necessary, British officers in the border region attacked Afghan positions. Inconclusive combat took place at scattered points along a wide front. For the British, the unreliability of their native contingents proved only one of several unsettling discoveries in a messy, unpopular, and unsatisfactory campaign. At a time when it could ill afford the money, the British Government of India was obliged to increase its budget by an enormous sum of 14,750,000 pounds to cover the costs of the one-month campaign.

Afghan Independence

Although they succeeded in expelling the Afghan forces from India and, by the end of May, had gained the upper hand, the British forces were inadequate to the task of invading, subduing, and occupying the Afghan kingdom. What won the day for them was the use of airplanes, which the tribesmen, with their primitive weapons, were unable to combat. In particular, it was the bombing of Afghan cities by the Royal Air Force that unnerved Amanullah and led him to ask for peace. Nonetheless, the outcome of the war, from the Afghans' point of view, was better than a draw. They had withdrawn from India but had regained their freedom within their own frontiers.

The Treaty of Rawalpindi, signed the morning of 8 August 1919, brought the Third Afghan War to an end. In the treaty Britain conceded the complete independence of Afghanistan, and relinquished control over Afghanistan's foreign relations.

A Traveler's Account of Afghanistan

By Frederick Simpich

In the early twentieth century, a European traveler disguised himself as a Muslim pilgrim and gave himself the name "Haji Mirza Hussein." He wanted to travel through Afghanistan and get an insider's view of the country. In the following account, first published in 1921, journalist Frederick Simpich describes some of the observations "Hussein" made during his travels, including many details about the rule of the Afghan emir Amanullah Khan. Simpich writes that the emir has attempted to keep Afghanistan isolated from the outside world, not even allowing railways or telegraph lines to connect the country to other nations. Only on very rare occasions is a European or American visitor permitted to visit the country, Simpich notes. (Recent historians, however, argue that in fact Amanullah modernized Afghanistan, increased trade with Europe and Asia, and advanced a constitution that called for equal rights and individual freedoms.) Simpich also describes the caravan trade in Afghanistan and the strict regulations on foreigners who bring goods to the border to sell. Simpich argues that despite Afghanistan's imposed isolation, it is inevitable that the country will one day again become a battleground for other powerful countries. Frederick Simpich was a reporter for National Geographic.

T he buffer state of Afghanistan, historic shock-absorber between Great Britain and Russia in middle Asia, years ago put up a "Keep Out" sign, a "This Means You" warning, to all white men and Christians. The land is "posted"— to use a poacher's phrase—posted against trade and concession hunters, against missionaries, and against all military and political hunters in particular.

Frederick Simpich, "Everyday Life in Afghanistan," *National Geographic*, January 1921, pp. 85–110.

Time and again the British have pushed up from India to invade this high, rough region hard by the "roof of the world." More than once their envoys have been massacred or driven back, or imprisoned, with their wives and children, in the frowning, gloomy citadel of Kabul; and once a retreating white army "shot it out" almost to a man, scattering its bones all the way from Kabul back to the Indian frontier.

In sheer drama, in swift, startling action, in amazing, smashing climax, no chapter in all the tales of the romantic East is more absorbing than this story of Britain's wars with the Afghans. And Russians, too, in the splendid glittering days of the Tsars, waged their fierce campaigns from the North, over the steppes of Turkestan, with wild Cossack pitted against wary Afghans.

"Keep Out"

But the "Keep Out" sign is still up. Today [at the beginning of the twentieth century] the foreigner is no more welcome in Afghanistan than he was a hundred years ago. Forbidden Lhasa [Tibet] itself is no more exclusive than brooding, suspicious Kabul, the capital of this isolate, unfriendly realm of fanatic tribes, of rocks, deserts, irrigated valleys, and towering unsurveyed ranges.

No railways or telegraph lines cross this hermit country or run into it, and its six or seven million people are hardly on speaking terms with any other nation.

Night and day, from stone watchtowers and hidden nooks along the ancient caravan trails that lead in from India, from Persia and Russia—trails used long ago by Alexander [the Great, Macedonian emperor] and Jenghiz Khan [a Mongol emperor]—squads of bearded, turbaned Afghans, with imported field glasses and long rifles, are keeping watch against trespassers from without.

For reasons of foreign policy, the Amir [Amanullah Khan] has long felt the necessity of secluding his little-known land to the greatest possible extent from the outside world. Only a few Europeans, mostly British, but occasionally also an American and now and then a few Russians or Germans, have had permission to come into this country and to sojourn for a while in its curious capital. But even on such rare occasions as when a foreign engineer, or a doctor whose services are badly needed, is admitted by the grace of the Amir, the visitor is subject to a surveillance that amounts almost to imprisonment.

No ambassadors or ministers, not even missionaries, are permitted to reside in this forbidden Moslem land. "Splendid isolation" is a sort of Afghan tradition, a conviction that the coming of the foreigner will spell the end of the Amir and his unique, absolute rule.

The Undisputed Authority of the Amir

Today [1921] no other monarch anywhere wields such undisputed authority or is in closer touch with the everyday life of his subjects. He personally runs his country's religion, its foreign affairs, and he even supervises much of its commerce. He also owns and censors the only newspaper printed in all Afghanistan. Incidentally, he keeps 58 automobiles, and he *never* walks. Even from one palace to another, he goes by motor over short pieces of road built especially for his pleasure.

From the [First] World War, though he took no active part in it, the Amir emerged with singular profits. His old and once rival neighbors, Great Britain and Russia, drawn together as allies in the world conflict, left him a free hand, and in 1919 Great Britain officially recognized the political independence of this much-buffeted buffer state, to whose rulers she had so long paid a fat annuity.

With an area of 245,000 square miles, Afghanistan is, next to Tibet, the largest country in the world that is practically closed to the citizens of other nations. But political life at wary, alert Kabul is in sharp contrast to the meditative seclusion and classic aloofness of the pious lamas at Lhasa.

Amir Amanullah Khan, through his agents in India and elsewhere, is in close touch with the world's current events; and, as the last remaining independent ruler of a Moslem country, now that the flower of the Caliph at Stamboul is broken [i.e., the Ottoman Empire has collapsed], he wields a far-reaching influence throughout the Mohammedan [Moslem] world; also, because his land happens to lie just as it does on the map of the world, it is plain that for a long time to come he will be an active force in the political destinies of middle Asia. Like Menelik of Abyssinia, Queen Lil of the Hawaiian Islands, or the last of the Fiji kings, this Amir, remote and obscure as his kingdom is, stands out in his time as a picturesque world figure.

The Amir's word, his veriest whim, is law to his millions of subjects. He is, in truth, the last of the despots, a sort of modern Oriental patriarch on a grand scale. His judgments are, of course, based primarily on the Koran, or on the common law of the land; for there is no statute book, no penal code, and no court.

To keep the wires of politics, of military and economic control, in his own hands, the Amir vests subordinate authority only in his relatives and close friends; and woe betide the incautious underling who dares think for himself or act contrary to the Amir's wishes; for in this primitive, secluded region there still survive many unique and startling methods of "rendering a culprit innocuous."

The Amir reserves to himself the right of passing death sentences. The cruel Afghan forms of punishment, such as shooting a prisoner from the cannon's muzzle, sabering off his head, ston-

AMANULLAH'S REFORMS

Amanullah Khan, emir of Afghanistan from 1919 to 1929, interacted with Western leaders and was eager to bring his country into the modern world. He ambitiously set about making many kinds of reforms. However, tribal and religious leaders resisted these efforts. The following excerpt describes some of Amanullah's reforms.

Amanullah's domestic reforms were no less dramatic than his initiatives in foreign policy, but the king's achievement of complete independence was not matched by equally permanent gains in domestic politics. The great Afghan intellectual and nationalist, Tarzi, was Amanullah's father-in-law, and he encouraged the monarch's interest in social and political reform. Tarzi, however, urged gradual reform built on the basis of a strong army and central government, as had occurred in Turkey under Mustafa Kemal (Atatürk), who offered to send Turkish officers to train the royal army. Amanullah, however, was unwilling to put off implementing his ideas. His reforms touched on many areas of Afghan life, but among the first (and perhaps the most important) were those that affected the army.

Although Amanullah has been accused of neglecting the army and of trying to strip it of its power, the foremost scholar of this period, Poullada, concludes that the king was

ing him to death, burying him alive, cutting off his hands and feet or putting out his eyes, are seldom employed nowadays; yet often the criminal himself will choose a quick though violent exodus to paradise rather than suffer long imprisonment in a filthy iron cage, perhaps to die eventually of starvation.

The way of the transgressor in Afghanistan continues to be uncommonly hard, however. Time and again, in the recorded history of this land, deposed amirs, troublesome relatives, and political enemies have been deliberately blinded, there being a tradition here that no man with any physical affliction may hold a public office of honor or profit.

---

simply trying to cast the army in a different mold. It was under Amanullah, for instance, that in 1921 the Afghan air force was established, based on a few Russian planes and pilots; Afghan personnel later received training in France, Italy, and Turkey. . . .

Amanullah's reforms—if fully enacted—would have totally transformed Afghanistan. Most of his proposals, however, died with his abdication. Among the social and educational reforms were the adoption of the solar calendar; requirement of Western dress in parts of Kabul and a few other areas; discouragement of the veiling and seclusion of women; abolition of slavery and forced labor; introduction of secular education, including education for girls; adult education classes; and education for nomads.

Political and judicial reforms were equally radical for the time and included Afghanistan's first constitution (1923); guarantee of civil rights (first by decree and then in the constitution); universal national registration and issuance of identity cards; establishment of a legislative assembly; creation of a court system and of secular penal, civil, and commercial codes; prohibition of blood money; and abolition of subsidies and privileges for tribal chiefs and the royal family.

From Sally Ann Baynard, "Historical Setting," in *Afghanistan: A Country Study*, ed. Richard F. Nyrop and Donald M. Seekins. Washington, DC: U.S. Government Printing Office, 1986.

From the Persians the Afghans got the idea of marrying more than one wife; but, like the Persians, too, they have found, to their dismay, that polygamy is nowadays more expensive than exciting.

Sometimes, when the Amir wants to favor his faithful officials with presents, or perhaps to play practical jokes in certain cases, he distributes women among them; but these "gifts" often prove so troublesome that no great degree of gratitude is apparent among the recipients.

Amir Habibullah Khan [Amanullah's father] (who was assassinated in 1919) had a harem of over one hundred women, and among these, strangely enough, were a few Europeans. The present Amir, Amanullah Khan, has but one wife.

Caravan Trade

The trade of Afghanistan is moved entirely by caravans and is largely in the hands of Hindus and Tadjiks. The chief route lies through the famous Khyber Pass, the great gateway from India, which has been fortified by the British Government. This pass is open every week, on Tuesdays and Fridays, except in very hot weather, when it is available to trade only on Fridays. A most rigid scrutiny is exercised by the Amir's agents on all who come and go. As soon as caravans from India enter the country, their Indian leaders are turned back and heavily armed Afghan guides take their places.

Some of these Afghan caravans, organized with military precision, number thousands of camels and a proportionate number of guides and camel-drivers. In the morning the Khyber Pass is open for caravans coming into Afghanistan, and in the afternoon for those routed in the opposite direction. The pass is absolutely closed between sundown and sun-up.

Camels leaving the country are usually loaded with wool, skins, dried fruits and vegetables, assorted gums, and spices. Thousands of horses are also driven along for sale in India as cavalry and polo mounts.

Supplying the wants of the Amir and his court is an interesting undertaking and is usually accomplished by his own agents, who reside in the cities of India. All goods consigned to him come in duty free; he buys anything that strikes his fancy, and often amuses himself by studying the pictures in mail-order catalogues.

The Yankee fountain pen and cheap watch are popular in Kabul. Most imports, however, come from India and China. Of late much Japanese merchandise is finding its way into the country. Either directly or through reshipping, India supplies Afghanistan with cotton goods, hardware, sugar and tea, dye materials, and silver bars for the coining of money. Gun running and the smuggling of ammunition, which flourished for many years, have recently been restricted by British supervision of the Indian frontiers. Though camels and packhorses, *yabus*, are mostly used for transport, it is not at all uncommon to see elephants, and even wheelbarrows, on the Afghan trails.

Owing to the aggressive pursuit and harsh punishment meted out by the Amir's troops, the once famous robbers of the Afghan hills have almost disappeared, so that caravans, even in the desert districts, can now travel in safety; but in some provinces near the borders constant quarrels and raids are going on among hostile tribes.

A Colorful Military

In military matters, Turkish influence is noticeable, and Turkish officers are used as instructors. In all Asia no fighting force is more picturesque or presents a more astonishing mixture of ancient and modern fighting methods than does the army of the Amir. Most of his troops are mounted, either on horses or camels, and a few of his better regiments of cavalry are organized somewhat after the Anglo-Indian style. The regulars are recruited mostly from among the town-dwelling Tadjiks.

The Malkis, or territorials, are organized and used in the various provinces as a sort of home guard. Some of them use flintlocks, and many depend on the spear and the long, curved sword for dispatching an enemy at close quarters. This army is about 70,000 strong. Save a few field howitzers and mountain guns it has no artillery.

Afghanistan's willful isolation of herself has, of course, affected the life of her people. Even among the different tribes within the country, jealousies and ethnological differences are conspicuous. The high mountains and frequent deserts so separate the cultivated and inhabited districts that tribal customs and habits, tongues, and religious differences are found here in sharper contrast than in most other countries of the East.

The Amir keeps at Peshawar a political agent, who occasionally pays a visit to the Viceroy of India; and, since Afghanistan's formal independence of 1919, envoys have been sent to Persia and one is perhaps now in Soviet Russia.

But because of the Afghan's chronic aversion to all foreigners, and the clever exclusion policy of the Amir, aided by nature's own barriers of sand wastes and almost inaccessible mountain ranges, it is likely that for a long time to come foreign influence will spread but slowly in this isolated land.

Yet the Amir and his military aristocracy follow intently all big events in the turbulent outside world. America is spoken of with sympathy and admiration, and, despite the prevailing illiteracy, many Afghans display an amazing knowledge of geography and current history. During the World War even the nomads on the steppes had fairly accurate news of great battles, and they had heard of air raids and submarines.

Today all Islam is in ominous ferment. Though the World War is officially ended, fights and disputes are still sweeping over Asia. Eventually and inevitably Afghanistan must again become the object of rivalry among big powers that rub shoulders in the East.

The Rise and Fall of Communism in Afghanistan

Afghan Resistance to Communism

By Thomas T. Hammond

Following the time of the Great Game, the nineteenth-century contest between the Russians and the British over who should wield influence and power over Afghanistan, the Afghans developed a love-hate relationship with Russia and its successor, the Soviet Union. For decades the Soviet Union provided various kinds of aid to Afghanistan, including help building roads and training and education for many Afghan citizens. Perhaps as a consequence of that education, an Afghan Communist movement began to gain influence in the 1960s. The Communist People's Democratic Party of Afghanistan (PDPA) was founded in 1965 and soon held several government seats. The PDPA overthrew the government of Mohammad Daud in 1978 and instituted land reforms, implemented state control of the economy, and developed literacy and medical programs. However, many people opposed the new government. They believed that Marxism, with its rejection of religion, would undermine their practice of Islam. They also resented Soviet influence over the Afghan government. The following article by Thomas T. Hammond describes the PDPA's efforts to enforce a Communist system of government and the massive resistance of the Afghan people. Hammond is the author of The Anatomy of Communist Takeovers, Witnesses to the Origins of the Cold War, *and* Red Flag over Afghanistan.

The assumption of power by the communists [in 1978] was followed by a series of purges, imprisonments, and executions. Thousands of [president Mohammad] Daoud's civil servants, diplomats, governors, professors, army officers, police, and the like were thrown into jail, and their positions were taken over by party faithful with few qualifications and little experience. Next came the turn of the [communist faction] Parcham leaders. . . .

Thomas T. Hammond, *Red Flag over Afghanistan: The Communist Coup, the Soviet Invasion , and the Consequences.* Boulder, CO: Westview Press, 1984. Copyright © 1984 by Westview Press, Inc. Reproduced by permission of the author's estate.

General Abdul Qader, one of the two top leaders of the coup,[1] had been rewarded with the post of minister of defense, but in August [1978] he was charged with engaging in a conspiracy and was locked up. With him went the chief of staff of the army, the minister of public works, the minister of planning, the minister of frontier affairs, and, in the weeks that followed, numerous other lesser figures.

One of the greatest problems in Afghanistan always had been a shortage of trained, capable administrators to run the government and the economy. With the purge—first, of the top officials from the Daoud regime, then of the Parchamis, and finally of all the others who were suspected of being anticommunist—the lack of competent personnel became acute. Young party members with no training or experience suddenly became deputy ministers, managers of state enterprises, or chairmen of state committees, much to the disgust of older bureaucrats with long years of service. It is no wonder, then, that the government had difficulty in planning and carrying out its program of reforms.

The Communist Reform Program

There seems to be no reason to doubt that the [communist faction] Khalq leaders sincerely wished to institute a number of desirable and long-overdue reforms—to improve the lot of the peasants, elevate the status of women, eliminate racial discrimination, wipe out backwardness, and make Afghanistan a modern, prosperous state. But good intentions are not enough. As has happened in other communist countries, the attempt to impose rapid and arbitrary change by brute force, against the wishes of the people, produced not progress but chaos, bloodshed, and civil war.

[Khalq leader Noor Mohammad] Taraki realized that he would have to use force to carry out his program, as he indicated in an interview with *Die Zeit:*

> ZEIT: Are not you and your government running the risk of asking too much of the traditional and conservatively Islamic people of Afghanistan?
>
> TARAKI: The people will follow us out of conviction or out of fear of punishment. We do not want to overhas-

1. On April 27, 1978, Afghan troops backing the Communist Party seized the capital and murdered Daoud in the presidential palace.

ten our reforms; we want to implement them step by
step. Yet, we will not be able to do that completely
without applying some force.

Taraki did use force, as he said he would. He also "overhas-
tened" his reforms, and he failed to pay enough attention to social and economic conditions in Afghanistan. [According to
scholar Anthony Hyman,] the attempt by Taraki and [Hafizul-
lah] Amin to introduce an Afghan form of socialism, "violated
practically every Afghan cultural norm, and strayed far beyond
the allowable bounds of deviance in the social, economic, and
political institutions. It almost appears that they systematically
planned to alienate every segment of the Afghan people."

Land Reform

Taraki, Amin, and many other Khalq leaders came from rural
backgrounds, and one would have expected them to understand
the attitudes, traditions, and customs of the peasants, but they did
not. This is illustrated by the land reform decreed in November
1978. The official press gave the impression that in every village
the reform was [as Hyman notes] "a great success, with peasants
dancing for joy, kissing the deeds of ownership, and waving aloft
the red flag of the ruling Khalq party."

But in fact the reform seems to have existed mostly on paper,
for several reasons: First, the young, inexperienced bureaucrats
(many of them city boys) who were sent into the countryside to
implement the reform did not understand the complications of
rural relationships and were not trusted either by the landlords or
the peasants. Second, many of the peasants refused to accept the
land, either because they were afraid of the landlords, were kinsmen of the landlords, or because, according to Muslim law, private property cannot be taken from another without compensa-
tion. Third, implementation of the reform was hindered by the
lack of accurate statistics on landownership or population.
Fourth, the would-be reformers tried to apply a crude version of
Marxist class relations to a society that was organized in a different way. The main divisions in Afghan society are not by class,
but by "household, lineage, clan, tribe, settlement or village and
ethnic group" [according to Richard S. Newell in *Revolution and
Revolt in Afghanistan*]. Fifth, land ownership was linked to traditions of local autonomy. "Afghan khans and other local leaders

are expected to protect their clients from intrusions by the central government. Hence institutions of land control, tenancy and labour service are often linked to the performance of local leaders in maintaining local autonomy on the basis of consensus within the community" [Newell writes]. As a result the communists who arrived in the villages with copies of the land decree in their hands were often looked upon as representatives of the hated central government, trying to overthrow traditional methods of local self-government. Finally, it was impossible to carry out such a complex, nationwide reform when large parts of the country were in armed rebellion.

A State Department cable described the land reform as follows: "Many landless and 'land poor' peasants had wanted to refuse to accept land because of religious scruples or fear of future retribution by the deprived landlords. The *Khalqis* forced them to accept the land, threatening them with imprisonment if they refused. . . . Several of these peasants later committed suicide.". . .

After a few months, many of the government's agrarian measures, which had been introduced with much fanfare, were quietly dropped. The land distribution, combined with the civil war and the other "reforms," so disrupted Afghan agriculture that a previously self-sufficient country was faced with a large deficit of grain.

Other Reforms

Another reform that was enacted without sufficient attention to existing customs and practical results was the attempt to ease the burden of peasant indebtedness. A decree of July 1978 reduced or canceled all rural debts prior to 1974 and forbade lenders to collect usury in the future. While the aim of the reform was admirable, the communists did not anticipate the consequences. Traditionally, many peasants had to borrow each year in order to buy the seed grain, farm tools, and other items needed to plant and raise a crop. When the government outlawed interest, the money lenders no longer had any incentive to make loans. The regime announced that it was going to establish a credit system for the peasants, but failed to do so in time. As a result, peasants were unable to plant their crops, and agricultural production fell.

Opposition was also aroused by the decree of October 17, 1978, regarding women and marriage. It forbade "giving a woman in marriage in exchange for money in cash or commodity"—in other words, the practice of "bride price" [in the words of historian Hannah Negaran]. Here again the government tried to enforce an overly simple solution to a complex economic and social custom, ignoring the fact that when a girl got married, her family lost her labor and had to give a dowry, which was usually worth as much as the bride price. Once more the ideologues in Kabul clashed head-on with ancient custom, thereby antagonizing the very people they were trying to help. Similarly, the attempt to impose a minimum age for marriage, prohibit arranged marriages, limit divorce payments, and send girls to school with boys inevitably aroused the opposition of Afghan men, whose male chauvinism is as massive as the mountains of the Hindu Kush.

Preaching Atheism

The factor that probably did most to create antagonism toward the communist regime, however, was its identification with atheism. The people of Afghanistan are almost 100 percent Muslim, and they are known to be very devout. The communist leaders repeatedly denied that they were communist, Marxist, or atheist, but few believed them. . . .

The masses soon saw that the Taraki/Amin regime was communist and that it intended to carry out religious policies similar to those in the Soviet Union—preaching atheism and discouraging religion. This was a fatal mistake on the part of the communists since "the judicial arm of the government was intertwined with Muslim ideology, and thus in the context of civil and criminal justice the government symbolized Islam" [as Amnesty International wrote]. So [as *Time* magazine observed in 1979] "the introduction of communist ideology and the debunking of Muslim beliefs in the schools . . . not only aroused the emotions of the tribes people against the Taraki/Amin regime, but also destroyed the foundation of the central government's legitimacy." To many Afghans, opposition to the communist regime became a religious duty.

The attitude of the common people toward the communists' religious policies is illustrated by the comment of an Afghan refugee:

> When the party workers came to our village, they . . .
> made jokes about us praying to Mecca five times a day
> and said we were backward. They said our Mullahs

were backward and that we should not pay attention to what they said anymore. They said our prayer beads were like chains to tie us, and they said our daughters should go to school with the boys, which is against our custom. They ordered books on Lenin and Marx and ordered that they be read, even though our Mullahs said that they should not be read.

Violations of Human Rights

The communist regime also antagonized people by its numerous executions. In a country where kinship is crucial, each execution embittered parents, brothers and sisters, aunts and uncles, cousins—indeed, all relatives and all members of the tribe. In Afghanistan there is a strong tradition that the killing of a relative must be avenged by the death of those responsible. Thus the regime created for itself a large mass of Afghans who felt that it was their familial duty to fight against the communists. The contrast between the policies of the Daoud regime and those of the communist regime regarding executions is worth noting: While many of the members of the communist government spent time in jail under Daoud, they survived, but Daoud, his family, and thousands of others are dead, the victims of communist executioners.

Aside from executions, the Taraki/Amin regime incurred enmity among the people by mass arrests and torture. Amnesty International issued a report in November 1979 that accused the government of holding 12,000 prisoners in Pul-i-Charkhi prison in Kabul, a facility designed for 6,000 persons. Among them, the report said, were 42 women and children whose only crime was that they were relatives of political prisoners. Those incarcerated included people of all political views, from Muslim fundamentalists to Marxists. Most of the prisoners, Amnesty International reported, were held without charges and without trial, and many of them had been tortured. The torture had included "severe beatings, whippings, pulling out of prisoner's nails, burning his hair, and sleep deprivation." *Time* magazine claimed in October 1979 that the regime had imprisoned 30,000 people and executed 2,000 others.

To sum up the domestic program of the Taraki/Amin regime, one might say that a small elite of incompetent urban ideologues with no practical experience in governing and with little tolerance for native customs attempted by force to introduce alien and ill-conceived reforms, even though the regime had few capable administrators and little popular support. Moreover, these ideologues tried to introduce the reforms overnight, while at the same time they offended the religious beliefs and tribal traditions of the majority of the population. If the communists had set out deliberately to make themselves hated, they could hardly have done a more thorough job.

The People Rise Up in Rebellion

With the communist government attempting to enforce such unpopular policies, it is not surprising that opposition developed, and since Afghans have a long tradition of fighting for their rights, the opposition inevitably took the form of armed revolt. At first there was little opposition because the people didn't know much about the new regime, and the government hadn't yet had time to carry out its new policies. A cable from the American Embassy in Kabul described the situation as follows:

> For a few months, at least, following the 1978 revolution, most Afghans—rural as well as urban dwellers . . . were clearly willing to give the *Khalqis* the benefit of the doubt and see what their policies would be. Although the *Khalqis* were not universally welcomed within the country, Daoud's demise was not overly mourned, and in the Afghan tradition most were ready to tolerate any type of central government as long as that government stuck to its own turf and posed no threat to the time-honored Afghan ways of life.

But already in the summer of 1978 there were uprisings in Nuristan and Badakhshan, and in the following months the revolt spread until it involved every one of the twenty-nine provinces and almost all of the ethnic groups in Afghanistan. The rebellion was spurred on in part by Muslim leaders, who proclaimed a *jihad*—a holy war—against the godless communists, but the people found many things about the regime to object to besides its atheism. Chief among these was the attempt by Kabul to violate the centuries-old tradition of autonomy, of self-rule by the people themselves and by their customary local leaders. The communist bureaucrats meddled in the local affairs in numerous obnoxious ways, offensive to almost everybody. As a result, the opposition included not only mullahs, khans, landlords, merchants, and moneylenders, but all classes of the population. The revolt also cut across ethnic divisions. Indeed, some tribes that for centuries had fought each other, now united to fight against the communists.

As the insurrection got into full swing, the territory under the regime's control shrank. In some areas government troops held sway during the daytime, while *mujaheddin* (holy warriors) dominated the scene at night. Even major highways were subject to frequent raids, so that trucks had to be sent in convoys, guarded by tanks. In general, the rebels controlled the countryside and the villages, while the government dominated the cities. But in March 1979 Afghan soldiers in Herat, a major city, joined with rebels in a bloodbath that led to the killing of many government officials and loyal soldiers, as well as a number of Soviet advisers and their families. The Soviet citizens were beheaded, their heads stuck on pikes and paraded around the city. The government bombed and strafed Herat with jets and helicopters, but was unable to restore order until hundreds, perhaps thousands, had been killed. In Kabul itself there were demonstrations, strikes, protests, bombings, assassinations, and at least two mutinies.

The Unreliable Afghan Army

The Afghan army proved to be a highly unreliable tool for suppressing the rebellion because units often refused to fight, retreated under fire, or deserted, taking their weapons with them. Indeed, the rebels claim that their main source of arms, particularly modern arms like rockets and antitank guns, has been from Afghan troops. In August 1979 soldiers in the Bala Hissar barracks in Kabul mutinied, and fighting continued for hours before loyal troops were able to bring them under control. As rebellion spread throughout the country, the government needed more soldiers, so it increased draft quotas; this in turn led to more revolts. According to Professor R. Lincoln Keiser, the attempt to increase conscription in Darra-i-Nur was a major reason for the rebellion in that area.

Faced with growing resistance, government forces retaliated with ruthless counterattacks. Since they often could not control the ground, they relied on their superiority in the air. Villages were strafed and bombed—sometimes with napalm—in an attempt to demolish completely those villages that harbored rebel forces. In addition, the communists deliberately destroyed farm crops in an attempt to starve the people into submission. These brutal methods simply drove more peasants into the ranks of the opposition.

Resistance grew also because many people considered the communist leaders to be puppets of the Russians. Afghans have long looked upon the Russians with dislike. If a Russian came into an Afghan shop, it sometimes happened that the shopkeeper would refuse to wait on him or would do so in a surly manner. . . .

As the rebellion grew and the communist regime showed itself less and less able to suppress it, the Soviets were forced to increase their role in the conflict. More Soviet military personnel were sent in to advise the Afghan forces until, by the middle of November 1979, there were perhaps as many as 4,500 advisers in the country. In addition, increased supplies of modern military equipment were sent to Afghanistan, and Soviet pilots began flying helicopter gunships and jet fighters in attacks on the rebels. The Soviets also sent a special unit of airborne troops to assume control of Bagram airfield, the important military base north of Kabul. Step by step, Moscow was moving in the direction of a massive invasion.

The Soviet Invasion of Afghanistan

By Larry P. Goodson

In 1973 Mohammad Daud seized power in a military coup and declared Afghanistan a republic. He named himself president and prime minister and began instituting economic and social reforms. However, his efforts were opposed by both the conservative Muslims and the Afghan Communists who had slowly been making inroads into Afghanistan's government since 1965. Daud was overthrown in 1978, and Nur Mohammad Taraki, a member of the Communist People's Democratic Party of Afghanistan (PDPA), became the new president. The PDPA had difficulty maintaining power and requested help from the Soviet Union to maintain control. Despite Soviet aid, the Afghan government was unable to suppress the rebels. In 1979 the Soviets launched a full-fledged invasion, joining the Afghan government forces in combating the resistance fighters. The invasion became an unwinnable ten-year war in which more than fifty thousand Soviet soldiers and 2 million Afghans lost their lives. Finally, in 1989 the Soviets withdrew their troops from Afghanistan. However, the man the Soviets had supported as president, Mohammad Najibullah, remained in office. The following selection by Larry P. Goodson describes the events leading up to the Soviet invasion. Goodson is an associate professor of international studies at Bentley College in Waltham, Massachusetts, and the author of Afghanistan's Endless War, Middle East Politics, *and* The Talibanization of Pakistan.

The Afghan War began with the communist coup d'etat by officers in the army and air force on April 27, 1978. This event, now known as the Saur Revolution, developed out of unrest on both sides of the political spectrum over [president Mohammad] Daoud's policies. [According to scholar Henry S.

Larry P. Goodson, *Afghanistan's Endless War: State Failure, Regional Politics, and the Rise of the Taliban.* Seattle: University of Washington Press, 2001. Copyright © 2001 by the University of Washington Press. Reproduced by permission.

Bradsher] religious traditionalists were unhappy with his "modernization and centralization of authority, which threatened villagers' virtual autonomy." The PDPA [People's Democratic Party of Afghanistan], whose bitterly antagonistic factions Khalq and Parcham had ended their ten-year split in a unification conference in July 1977, resented the steady erosion of its position that Daoud's distancing from the Soviet Union had caused.

The new government enjoyed a honeymoon period that for most of the country lasted through the summer of 1978. The summer months were a busy time for the predominantly rural Afghans. Their traditional pattern of local rebellion to express displeasure with government began after the fall harvest. Also, the communists moved slowly in the beginning, focusing first on intraparty squabbles. In July 1978, after a rapprochement of one year, Khalq and Parcham split again. The first of a series of purges sent Babrak Karmal and other senior Parchamis abroad as ambassadors. Open violence was kept to a minimum, however, and the independent-minded Afghan villagers ignored the promulgated reforms. No effort was made to suppress Islam; instead, government officials made a public effort to embrace it.

Bitter Reaction to Communist Reforms

This moderate approach was somewhat successful, but in late October a series of sweeping reform policies wiped out all previous progress. A disastrous symbolic move occurred with the introduction of the new national flag in October; the traditional Islamic green was replaced by communist red. It was quickly followed by new policies regarding land reform, credit reform, marriages, and mandatory education for both sexes. Young officials were sent to the countryside to implement these reforms. As [historians] Richard and Nancy Newell noted:

> Any one of these programs, tactlessly introduced, would almost certainly have aroused a bitter reaction among most segments of the population. When they were introduced together as a package under the red banner of communism, the effect was catastrophic. . . . Taken together, these reforms virtually guaranteed opposition. Their enforcement . . . was brought home by government servants who saw no virtue in using tact or diplomacy. Incidents of protest quickly mushroomed into local armed revolts.

These reforms struck at the very heart of the socioeconomic structure of Afghanistan's rural society; indeed, their sudden nationwide introduction, with no preliminary pilot programs, suggests that this was their real purpose. The bases of authority in rural society were the family and the tribe or clan. Implementation of these reforms eroded the underpinnings of these bases of authority; consequently, it is hardly surprising that they were so fiercely resisted. When the Khalq regime signed a friendship treaty with the USSR in December 1978, it made clear under whose patronage the restructuring of Afghanistan would occur. Thereafter, the rebellion spread rapidly and unremittingly.

By early 1979, most of Afghanistan was in open revolt against the Khalq government. At least twenty-four of the (then) twenty-eight provinces of Afghanistan had suffered outbreaks of violence. The rebellion first developed in the Nuristan valleys of Kunar province in the summer of 1978. By the autumn of 1978, widespread resistance was occurring in the Tajik northeast and the central Hazarajat region. These pockets of earliest upheaval all appeared among oppressed minority populations whose resistance was motivated in part by traditional ethnic hostility toward the Pushtun-dominated government.

Open Revolt

Although the initial outbreaks of violence took place among the minorities, antigovernment activity spread rapidly among the Pushtuns, from whom the major early mujahideen groups developed. . . . Most of the leaders split off from Gulbuddin Hekmatyar's Hezb-i-Islami party and acquired the support of local fronts; some of these parties were looser coalitions than others. Pushtun activism was motivated by anger at the reform policies, abhorrence of the new government's manifestly anti-Islamic ideology, and desire for national liberation. By the spring of 1979, nationwide resistance to the Khalq regime had developed. Without the preexisting ethnic tensions and ill-timed government reform policies it is questionable whether the rebellion would have begun so suddenly or spread so vigorously. That it did led inexorably to the Soviet invasion.

In the early spring of 1979, war came to the cities of Afghanistan. In mid–March there was a general uprising in Herat. More than one hundred Soviets reportedly were hunted down and killed in savage violence that claimed three thousand to five thousand lives. Revolts and uprisings in other major cities quickly followed. In April, Afghan army units mutinied in Jalalabad, killing their Soviet advisers and refusing to fight the resistance. Many of these soldiers went over to the mujahideen, equipment in hand. Desertion, unwillingness to serve, and attrition reduced the Afghan Army; by the end of 1980 it had been reduced from eighty thousand to thirty thousand men.

The government in Kabul felt the pressure generated by the popular uprisings in the countryside, particularly the savage fighting in Herat and the defection of its troops in Jalalabad. In April Afghan government forces with Soviet advisers massacred 1,170 men and boys of Kerala village in Kunar, near the border with Pakistan. This atrocity became one of the best known in a war replete with atrocities, and it marked a clear deviation from the stylized tribal violence common less than a year earlier.

Although the conflict spread rapidly throughout Afghanistan, the Herat uprising in particular was responsible for two major developments. First, as Henry Bradsher argued, "Herat was a warning unheeded" that should have led the government to slow the pace of reform and attempt to win popular support. Instead, on March 27, 1979, the Khalq hard-liner Hafizullah Amin assumed the prime ministership and active control of the government, leaving Nur Mohammad Taraki as president and party leader but increasingly without power. The remaining Parchami elements in the government were purged as arrests and executions grew.

Soviets Accelerate Their Involvement

Second, the Soviets recognized that they must increase their level of involvement in Afghanistan if the PDPA government was to survive. Accordingly, more advisers and weapons poured into Kabul, some as early as March. The Soviets also began to prepare for a possible invasion. Elite officers and units were sent to Afghanistan, although publicly both governments asserted that the Afghans could take care of their own problems. On September 14, 1979, Amin ousted Takari, who was killed three weeks later on Amin's orders. Meanwhile, the Soviets' invasion preparations intensified as their dissatisfaction with the performance of the Kabul regime grew.

At the Politburo meeting of November 26, the Soviet leadership committed itself to the invasion of Afghanistan. On December 17 there was an assassination attempt on Amin's life, possibly with Soviet complicity. In response, Amin and some loyal troops moved to the Darulaman Palace on the outskirts of Kabul. If the Soviets had hoped to install Babrak Karmal after assisting another internal coup and assassination, they were now forced to consider another option. Bradsher summarized the Soviet frustration:

> [I]t must have been clear to Soviet leaders that their ef-
> forts to control the situation in Afghanistan had failed
> yet again. They had been unable to direct Afghan pol-
> icy . . . in the summer of 1979, they had failed to get
> rid of Amin and use Taraki as a more amenable leader
> in September, they had failed to rein Amin in during
> the autumn, and now they had failed to destroy him in
> a quiet, plausible way. . . . [I]t was time to . . . use brute
> force where diplomacy and conspiracy had failed.

Invasion

Shortly before midnight on December 24, Soviet troops started landing at the Kabul airport; they were followed by troop land-ings at the air bases at Bagram and Shindand and the airport at Kandahar. By Christmas morning of 1979 the Soviets were in Af-ghanistan. On December 27 the Soviet forces attacked Darulaman Palace. The citadel was overrun after a night of vicious fighting, including the use of poisonous gas to overcome the defenders, during which Amin was killed. By January 1, 1980, the Soviets had nearly eighty-five thousand soldiers in Afghanistan. They controlled the cities and government, and their puppet Karmal was in power. The initial invasion of Afghanistan was a success.

The Mujahideen Resist the Soviet Invasion

By Hamed Madani

In 1979 the Soviet Union invaded Afghanistan and installed a Communist regime headed by Babrak Karmal. However, many Afghans did not view Karmal as their legitimate leader and resisted the Karmal regime and the Soviet occupation. The Afghan resistance consisted of various tribal armies that, under normal circumstances, had little to do with each other and in many instances were competitors or even enemies. Now, facing a common foe, they managed to pull together to combat the Soviets and keep them sequestered in the cities. The resistance fighters, known as the mujahideen, or holy warriors, controlled the mountain areas that make up much of Afghanistan.

In the following selection Afghan writer Hamed Madani describes the Afghan resistance movement during the 1980s, including the role of the United States in supporting the mujahideen. At first the United States did not want to appear to be involved in the war against the Soviet occupiers and did not provide the fighters with U.S.-produced arms, Madani notes. In the mid-1980s, however, as information about the brutality of the Soviet occupation became well publicized, the United States began to openly support the mujahideen and supply them with American weapons. As Madani recounts, the Soviet Union was finally forced to withdraw from Afghanistan in 1989, but the mujahideen were not able to create a stable new government. Instead, Afghanistan entered a long period of civil war that led to the rise of the Taliban regime in the 1990s.

Hamed Madani is a professor of political science at Tarrant County College in Arlington, Texas. He has been writing and lecturing on Afghanistan politics and teaching American politics and foreign policy for more than twenty years. He is a native of Afghanistan.

Hamed Madani, *Afghanistan.* San Diego: Greenhaven Press, 2004. Copyright © 2004 by The Gale Group, Inc. Reproduced by permission.

Although President [Hafizullah] Amin was a Communist ally, the Soviet Union was becoming very alarmed at the unstable, unpredictable situation on its southern border. By 1979 the Amin government was on the verge of collapse, and the Soviets doubted he could control the country for much longer. They also feared that radical fundamental Islam growing inside of Afghanistan could take over as the prevailing ideology, as it had during the Islamic revolution in Iran that same year.

Afghanistan had also become an increasingly attractive economic and geopolitical resource to the Soviets, due to its proximity to Middle East oil reserves. The Soviet military was also gaining strength and wanted to directly experiment with its armed forces. The Soviets wanted to expose their units to real-life combat conditions and experience, and they believed that Afghanistan would be an ideal setting for that experience.

Taking into account all of these factors, the Kremlin [the Russian government] decided to use force to overthrow Amin and his regime. On December 25, 1979, some 115,000 Soviet troops invaded Afghanistan. Amin was toppled and murdered. Little is known how about he died, but some speculate that he was killed by a special Soviet commando unit while he was entertaining his guests at the opening of the new presidential palace in the outskirts of the capital. The USSR installed a new PDPA[1] regime headed by ex-Parcham[2] leader Babrak Karmal, who was brought into the country from exile by Soviet paratroopers during the invasion.

The pervasive Soviet presence in Afghanistan alienated wide segments of the population. Soviet soldiers patrolled the streets of Kabul and other major cities. They swept through villages, leaving mines in mosques and in the fields, some disguised as toys, that would kill civilians, especially curious children, when they tried to pick them up.

Although Babrak Karmal was formally in charge of the country, in reality the Soviets were in control. They dominated the bureaucracy by acting as military and civilian advisers to different governmental departments. Karmal, who ruled from 1980 to 1986, attempted to undo the Khalq's[3] reform programs in order

---

1. Afghanistan's Communist Party, the People's Democratic Party of Afghanistan   2. Parcham was a former faction of the PDPA.   3. The Khalq was a rival faction of the Parcham in the PDPA.

to win the support of the people. For example, he actively used Islam as a source of legitimacy for his regime by restoring the traditional Islamic colors of the Afghan flag and invoking the name of God before delivering his speeches to the nation. His government also announced that it would postpone the implementation of the Communist land reform program.

But Afghans viewed Karmal as merely a Soviet puppet and refused to grant his regime legitimacy. Instead, they resorted to continued resistance and violence against the Soviet occupation and the Karmal regime. Others fled to Pakistan and Iran and organized resistance groups against the government.

Resistance Movement

Organized resistance to the Soviet occupation took the form of a religious jihad or holy war—a war in defense of Islam against the atheist regime of Kabul. Those who fought on behalf of Islam became known as the mujahideen (freedom fighters). They became the heart of the organized resistance against the Soviet occupation. Their struggle was waged to free Afghanistan from communism and restore an Islamic government. They established their headquarters and bases in Peshawar, Pakistan, and were made up of seven military-political organizations (*tanzims*).

The United States condemned the Soviet invasion and considered it a threat to the rest of the region, especially the oil-producing states of the Middle East. The United States was also concerned about the spread of communism and the growing influence of the Soviet Union. In order to contain further Soviet expansion, the United States began to support the opposition in Afghanistan.

American president Ronald Reagan considered the situation in Afghanistan to be a valuable political opportunity in America's global conflict with the Soviet Union. He wanted to support the mujahideen in order to bog down the Soviet Union in a protracted conflict that would drain them of their resources and ultimately weaken them. In his State of the Union message before the members of Congress in February 1985, Reagan stated that America must support those who defied Soviet-supported aggression. He further stated that support for freedom fighters was self-defense for America.

This statement became known as the Reagan Doctrine. The purpose of the doctrine was to help free nations under Communist domination. To implement this doctrine in Afghanistan, Reagan signed the National Security Decision Directive 66, which called for American efforts to drive Soviet forces from Afghanistan by all means available.

The CIA and the Arab Afghans

The Central Intelligence Agency (CIA) was provided with several billion dollars to launch the largest covert operation it had ever undertaken. The goal was to help the mujahideen defeat communism in Afghanistan during the 1980s. The CIA also placed advertisements in newspapers and newsletters in the Arab countries motivating young Muslims to join the Afghan "holy war."

Those who answered these advertisements became known as the Arab Afghans. According to author Mark Huband, "At [the campaign's] height there were around fifteen thousand who came from Saudi Arabia, five thousand from Yemen, between three and five thousand from Egypt, two thousand from Algeria, around one thousand from the Gulf, a thousand from Libya, and several hundred from Iraqi Kurdistan." The most famous of these Arab Afghans was Osama bin Laden, who joined the mujahideen in 1986.

Until 1986 the Americans were careful not to supply the fighters with U.S.-made arms. The strategy was to minimize the appearance of American involvement in the early stage of the war against the Soviet occupying force. The CIA counterinsurgency experts, therefore, purchased Soviet-made weapons from Egypt, China, India, and Israel. The CIA used the Pakistani military intelligence service, Inter-Services Intelligence (ISI), to organize the resistance groups and supply them with arms. The ISI allocated the weapons among the seven Peshawar-based organizations, who in turn distributed them inside Afghanistan to local commanders.

When the ugly details of the Soviet occupation of Afghanistan became known worldwide, the United States decided that it was time to openly and directly support the opposition. Therefore, the United States supplied the mujahideen with American arms, including the shoulder-held, laser-guided, heat-seeking Stinger missiles. The Stinger missiles inflicted many casualties as they destroyed hundreds of government aircraft and helicopters.

The war in Afghanistan drained the Soviet Union of both its material and human resources. It cost the Soviet Union tens of billions of dollars and the lives of over fifteen thousand Soviet soldiers. The Kremlin leaders had failed in their efforts to consolidate the Communist regime in Afghanistan and realized their blunder in 1986 when Mikhail Gorbachev called Afghanistan "a bleeding wound." Eventually the Soviet Union was forced to sign the United Nations–sponsored Geneva Accords in April 1988. The signatories to the accords included the Afghan government, the Soviet Union, Pakistan, and the United States. Specifically, the accords required the Soviet Union to withdraw all its forces from Afghanistan by February 1989. The last Afghan Communist government and its leader, Najibullah Ahmedzai, continued to rule in the absence of the Soviet forces until 1992.

The mujahideen were not invited to the Geneva negotiations

RIVALRIES AMONG THE MUJAHIDEEN

The following excerpt describes some of the differences between the various groups of mujahideen in Afghanistan. These differences have led to extensive wars between the groups.

The resisters [of the Soviet invasion]—henceforth to call themselves and be known as *mujahideen*, or "those who fight the holy war" (*jihad*)—would not have been Afghans had they not found more to differ than agree over. Familiar tribal rivalries, often complicated by personal loyalties and antipathies, divided them. So, too, did religion and traditional political alignment. In all, some forty resistance groups have been identified. The most important, however, number six, equally divided between Islamic fundamentalism and Afghan traditionalism. . . .

The size and strength of these groups proves chronically difficult to estimate. It is commonly said that there are between 90,000 and 120,000 *mujahideen* of all parties in the field and that the number can rise to a quarter of a million during the height of the annual campaigning season. Such figures certainly square with the manpower known to be available [in 1985]. Nearly four million Afghans have now gone into exile—a million to Iran, the rest to Pakistan, where because the Geneva Accords dealt with the Soviet withdrawal and not the composition of the future government in Afghanistan. The mujahideen rejected the Geneva Accords and continued their resistance against the last Soviet-sponsored government of [Najibullah] Ahmedzai. By early 1992, due to lack of continued Russian military and economic support, the last Communist government collapsed. The mujahideen assumed power and declared the Islamic State of Afghanistan. The mujahideen agreed to create a broad-based temporary government and hold general elections within two years.

However, the mujahideen could not agree among themselves over the sharing of power and soon turned their guns against

they live in 300 camps in the North-West Frontier Province. These camps are also base areas for the *mujahideen*, from which the fighters regularly pass through Pakistani tribal territory and then onward across the frontier by any of the 200 passes that lead through the mountains. But not even the Pakistani government seems able to count heads, while the group leaders remain too divided to pool information about how many followers each has. Attempts to impose unity, sponsored particularly by fellow Moslems in the Middle East, have failed to secure peace even among the groups' headquarters in Peshawar, while from inside Afghanistan itself come regular reports of the *mujahideen* fighting each other, sometimes at the expense of waging the war against the Russians. Hezb and Jamiat, for example, have certainly fought bitterly, even though both are Islamic fundamentalist in creed; their antipathy is largely ethnic. In central Afghanistan, where the Hazara form the only sizable Shi'ite [Muslim] group in the resistance, the fighting that has taken place has been along traditionalist-fundamentalist lines. Such fighting is the despair of foreign supporters of the *mujahideen*, who periodically cut off aid and bang heads in an effort to make the *mujahideen* sink their differences.

John Keegan, "The Ordeal of Afghanistan," *Atlantic Monthly*, November 1985.

each other. As fighting among various groups of mujahideen escalated, Afghanistan became engulfed in civil war and was divided into several independent zones, each with its own warlord.

The civil war lasted for four years and had devastating consequences for the country. The capital was divided into zones of occupation, where competing factions of mujahideen occupied different parts of the city. The power struggle over the control of Kabul turned the city into armed camps. More than twenty-five thousand civilians lost their lives in Kabul alone. Government buildings, schools, mosques, and residential areas were utterly destroyed and Kabul was reduced to rubble. There was a shortage of food, electricity, and water. The battle for control of Kabul was a microcosm of what took place all over Afghanistan. Afghanistan's cities, which had been spared earlier destruction during the Soviet occupation, became the targets of the civil war. The country immersed itself in ethnic and religious violence, which led to further political fragmentation of Afghanistan.

Thus, the new game played between the United States and the Soviet Union in Afghanistan brought death and utter destruction to the country. During the civil war many Afghans lost their lives and several million Afghans abandoned their homes and went into exile in neighboring countries, mainly Pakistan and Iran. Major cities were completely destroyed. Although the mujahideen had recaptured their country from a major superpower and saved it from a dominant world ideology, they could not set aside their religious and ethnic differences and work toward a unified national government. As a result, the Afghan state once again collapsed.

Afghanistan's Last Communist Leader

By Phillip Corwin

The withdrawal of the Soviet army from Afghanistan in 1989 did not bring about the immediate collapse of the Communist government in the capital city of Kabul. President Mohammad Najibullah, head of the Communist-allied People's Democratic Party of Afghanistan, remained in power in Kabul while the various mujahideen groups that had been fighting the Soviets contested control of the countryside. The mujahideen sporadically attacked the capital for more than two years without actually taking it.

In the spring of 1992 the leaders of three different mujahideen groups, Gulbuddin Hekmatyar, Ahmed Shah Massoud, and Abdul Rashid Dostum, formed a temporary alliance. Their intense dislike of Najibullah and his attempts to marginalize their authority gave them a common cause. Mujahideen armies came down from the hills surrounding Kabul, bombarding government buildings, markets, and army installations. On April 15, while hostile fighters bent on his destruction filled the city's streets, President Najibullah prepared to flee the capital under the protection of several United Nations officials. Accompanying him were Benon Sevan, the head of the UN mission, and Phillip Corwin, a UN officer. Najibullah was prevented from escaping from Kabul by Dostum, whose Uzbek troops seized the city's airport.

Corwin kept a diary of the events as they unfolded in 1992 and published the entries in his memoir Doomed in Afghanistan. *The following selection is an extract from Corwin's memoir about the fall of Kabul and Najibullah's failed attempt to escape. Najibullah took sanctuary in Kabul's UN compound and remained a virtual prisoner there until the Taliban captured Kabul in September 1996. The Taliban dragged Najibullah from the compound and hanged him from one of the light posts in the capital.*

Phillip Corwin, *Doomed in Afghanistan: A UN Officer's Memoir of the Fall of Kabul and Najibullah's Failed Escape*. New Brunswick, NJ: Rutgers University Press, 2003. Copyright © 2003 by Phillip Corwin. Reproduced by permission of Rutgers, The State University.

[15 April 1992]

The activity around me seems almost surreal. All this talk of disaster, of a capital about to fall, of air bases being captured, of perimeter defenses that don't exist, of soldiers changing allegiances, of wild dogs patrolling the streets at night. Yet the small world I move in from day to day seems quite safe. It is run by internationals and supported by local Afghans, a kind of settler colonialism in the cause of peace. And what stimulates the adrenaline here and now are hope and determination—positive forces; not anxiety, dread, danger.

In fact, I really don't feel threatened. Inconvenienced, yes, because my freedom of movement is restricted, and my living conditions are often less than elegant. But I don't feel threatened, physically afraid. I wonder how I seem to the Afghans I deal with every day: the generals, the servants, the interpreters. Privileged, no doubt. A source of hope, perhaps. A foreigner, for sure. Can they feel my positive energy? . . .

Afghanistan Is Doomed

Russia is a major concern for the U.S. at all times, because it is a nuclear power. South America, because of its proximity to the United States, is also a major concern. If its economies collapse, the U.S. will be flooded with more immigrants, and United States banks will lose billions of dollars in loans. The Middle East is always a concern for the United States because of oil, and because of strategic considerations; even if the oil fields in Arabia ran dry, the area would be important geopolitically. China is important. Japan is important. In fact, now that Russian troops are out of Afghanistan, Afghanistan's problems are quite low on the priority lists of the United States, NATO, and by extension, the UN. Those are the realities.

Then there is still debate about whether the UN has the right under the Charter to intervene *within* a country to protect threatened minorities. Military intervention needs some legal cover in order not to look like brazen imperialism. Can the international community use military force to protect the Kurds in Iraq, but not in Turkey? The Muslims in Bosnia, but not in China? Would it respond if the Uzbeks claimed they were a persecuted minority in Afghanistan? But these questions are academic now. Even if the UN Security Council did want to intervene militarily in Afghanistan, it would take the Council days to arrive at a decision, and months, under enormous risk, to bring in the necessary force, whereas Kabul is destined to fall within days. Afghanistan has effectively been abandoned by the international community, a case of political triage. It is doomed.

Massoud and Hekmatyar Threaten Kabul

At this point, [Northern Alliance commander Ahmed Shah] Massoud seems unstoppable. The question is, will [Hezb-i-Islami commander Gulbuddin] Hekmatyar accept Massoud's dominance, or will he choose to battle Massoud, either by taking Kabul or by circumventing the city and assaulting Massoud's positions to the north? And will Massoud enter Kabul, even though he has said he would not?

There is also the threat of ethnic and factional warfare within Kabul. Will the [Communist faction] Khalqi, who support [former president] Babrak Karmal, move against Najib's[1] people? The Khalqi are in Kabul. Some have never left, some have infiltrated among the refugees seeking asylum. Or, will the Pashtun in Kabul move against the non-Pashtun, whose refugees continue to swell Kabul, and who are virtually in control of certain neighborhoods?

Meanwhile, civil services have all but broken down. A few buses are running, but other services are spotty. Civil servants are not being paid. Like others, they are considering whether to defect, and if so, where to go, whom to join. This is what anarchy is all about—to feel a victim in your own home, in your own city, to have nobody to whom you can appeal, to feel you are a twenty-four-hour target for reasons that may exist only in the mind of an anonymous attacker, a neighbor, a former friend. *Things fall apart, the center cannot hold* (Yeats).

1030 hours. Briefing by [UN commander] Colonel Nowlan. Be sure that all vehicles are fueled, in good working order, and are flying a UN flag. When using radios, use only call signs and house numbers. No names. Be sure to know alternate routes to the airport in case we must evacuate. Bring a backpack to work, with enough to sustain you for a few days: socks, underwear, toiletries, clothes, raincoat, etc. Check *BBC* news every morning at 0500 and 0530. Everyone should have, or have access to, a short-wave radio.

We discuss where we will assemble for evacuation. There are

1. President Najibullah's nickname

several collection points. Each person is responsible for knowing his collection point.

1130 hours. Avni[2] and I go to visit [Afghan army commander] General Yar Mohammed. I have no idea what the general's responsibilities are, but at this point it doesn't matter. No one can exercise his responsibilities now. We simply stay in touch to see what information the general has.

He tells us that eleven of the fifteen members for the proposed Council of Impartials[3] were approved this morning in Peshawar. And there is a coalition government in Bagram, which fell yesterday to Massoud. No reports of violence there. No reports of arrests. A deal was struck.

Hekmatyar's forces are on the move to the south of Kabul. They may be assembling for an offensive on Kabul.

The general wants to do anything possible to prevent violence in Kabul. Massoud's forces, which took Charikar and Bagram, have said they had no intention of entering Kabul. He believes them. The problem is Hekmatyar. We have heard this refrain before, but each time we hear it again the speaker seems more desperate.

Desperation and Absurdity

Yesterday, the Afghan government decided to establish contact with forces to the north, loosely known as the Coalition of the North, or the Northern Alliance, an alliance between Massoud and [militia commander Abdul Rashid] Dostom. Today official directives will be released saying that government forces should join the predominantly mujahidin forces to the north, in order to prevent bloodshed, and to promote the UN peace plan.

[The real alliance, I think, has been between desperation and absurdity. Imagine: a government directive ordering its troops to desert and join the enemy, in order to promote a peace plan that the enemy has already rejected. And who will enforce the UN peace plan? A handful of unarmed UN military observers?]

Last night, General Yar Mohammed continues, the executive committee of the Watan (Homeland) Party decided that government forces should not take military action without direct orders from the president [who has already announced his intention to

---

2. Avni Botsal, a Turkish diplomat, served as deputy to UN head of mission Benon Sevan.   3. a group of opposition leaders prepared to serve as a transition government after the fall of Najibullah

resign, who has very little power outside of Kabul, and virtually no power within Kabul]. A group was sent to contact General Massoud to tell him that plans for air strikes against the Northern Alliance have been canceled. [Now that Bagram Air Base has been captured by Massoud, how could government planes carry out an air strike anyhow? Where would they fly from? And who would fly the planes? The pilots have deserted.]

The general says that once agreement on a number of issues has been reached with the Northern Alliance, the government will attempt to make agreement with forces to the east and south of the capital. These forces are largely responsible to Hekmatyar. Meanwhile, General Azimi is in charge of the defense of Kabul.

Last night half a dozen rockets were launched toward Kabul by Hekmatyar's forces. General Yar Mohammed says he hopes this will not be the beginning of a siege of Kabul. He sincerely hopes that Mr. [Benon] Sevan [head of the UN mission in Afghanistan] will be able to bring about a peaceful settlement to this conflict. The general would be quite happy if the same arrangement could be made for Kabul that was made for the northern cities. There should be a coalition between government forces and forces of the Northern Alliance. No bloodshed, no revenge.

[Of course we do not know that there has been no bloodshed in the northern cities, but I suspect it is true. Massoud is a very good politician and has numerous reasons for not punishing government troops. First of all, government forces are mostly "grunts," or conscripts, with no particular obligation to Najibullah. Massoud would rather have them as allies than as corpses. As for the officer corps, they know very well how the war is going, and they are quite willing to surrender. Besides, most of the government forces are Pashtun, and if Massoud starts to execute Pashtun soldiers, then he invites retaliation against (his) own ethnic Tajiks, many of whom are seeking refuge within Kabul. But Massoud is as clever as he is charismatic. He wants allegiance more than revenge. He knows there are times when trust and respect can be more a source of power than weapons.]

General Yar Mohammed thinks a coalition between government forces and the Northern Alliance is already possible within certain districts in Kabul. In fact, negotiations are ongoing at this moment with that goal in mind. However, he fears a rivalry between Hekmatyar and Massoud. He heard that Hekmatyar had received orders last night from his political leaders in Peshawar to attack Massoud, but that his soldiers refused to obey the order. They didn't want more bloodshed. The international community must prevent military rivalries inside Kabul. Hekmatyar is dangerous.

Finally, General Yar Mohammed tells us that the government's minister of interior affairs has reached an agreement with leaders of the Khalqi, Karmal's followers, that they would participate in a coalition along with the Watan Party (Najib's party) and others. [I doubt if they reached agreement, or if they did, whether the agreement would be honored by either side.]

A Sea of Confusion

1500 hours. Meeting with the National Salvation Society. The general who greets us tells us of his concerns. [I could never have imagined so many generals in such a small country. Their names bob in a sea of confusion in my irreverent mind. I do not even know the name of the speaker.] Developments have occurred, he says, that he had expected would happen only *after* the peace process had begun. For example, government forces north of the capital have defected to Massoud. That alliance should have taken place only after the peace process had begun. Then that development would have been acceptable. Now it was merely a defection, a sign of disarray.

The government's army is completely demoralized. Conditions are very bad. Kabul authorities are not strong enough to control the situation. If the Council of Impartials arrives in Kabul, perhaps they can control the situation. Otherwise, anarchy. He fears that there are too many ethnic and political groups within Kabul to permit a deal to be struck as it was in the northern cities and in Bagram. At this point Hekmatyar is closer to Kabul airport than Massoud is. If Hekmatyar captures the airport [which is on the outskirts of the city], he will enter Kabul. And he will plunder it. He is ruthless.

Mr. Sevan must immediately meet with Massoud and with Hekmatyar, and convince them to halt their advances toward Kabul. He must announce his intention to do so before it is too late, even before he can make the necessary arrangements. There must be a declaration by the UN demanding that military action against Kabul cease at once.

Mr. Sevan should meet with General Azimi rather than with Najibullah at this point. General Azimi is in charge of the defense of Kabul. Azimi should make a public declaration that he supports the UN peace process.

I ask if there is any possibility of factional fighting within Kabul.

Yes! the general says. He fears violence from the followers of Karmal, the Khalqi. He has not heard about any deal between the interior minister and Karmal's group. He does not believe there was one.

That night, before I go to sleep, I tell Avni to be sure to wake me if there are critical developments. He says he will.

16 April 1992

0110 hours. Avni wakes me with a call. Says a car will come to pick me up in fifteen minutes. I have laid my clothes out ahead of time, so that I can leave on short notice. Went to sleep around 11 p.m. When the phone first rings, I am in the middle of a dream. I can't find the telephone. I have forgotten where the lights are. I have forgotten where I am. When I find the phone, I recognize Avni's voice. I splash water on my face to wake up. I check to make sure I have my ID, my notebook, and more than one pen.

Preparing to Leave

0130 hours. A UN car arrives. The driver takes me to OSGAP[4] headquarters. From there we leave immediately for Najib's residence. We arrive within minutes. Najib is wearing a dark gray, pinstriped suit, a businessman's attire, and smiling anxiously. He is accompanied by General Toukhi, his chief of staff. Toukhi has his wife and three children (two boys and one girl) with him. Najib is accompanied by his brother, a bodyguard, and a servant. In all, a party of nine, including Najib.

We go inside, and Avni and General Toukhi go to work immediately on the statement by Najib that will formally announce his promised resignation. They have been working on it for the past few days. They are finishing if off now. It will be short.

I sit with Najib while they work. Najib is gracious, effusive. His emotion gushes through his fractured English. Though he is anxious, he seems more beset by sadness than fear. He wants once again to make his case to me. He is sad to leave Afghanistan—the country he has loved, defended; the country of his birth, the

---

4. UN office of the secretary general in Afghanistan and Pakistan

country in which his children may never grow up, which he may never see again.

And he is angry. I can feel his anger. It is an earthquake trapped in a jewel box, waiting to erupt. He is being driven out by extremists, barbarians, conspirators, religious fundamentalists. Afghanistan is being betrayed by feudal, medieval warlords in the pay of foreign rulers. The future is being swallowed by the past. He was the keystone that held together the arch that is Afghanistan as the country moved, perhaps too quickly, from feudalism to secular modernism. And now, he fears, the country will retreat into anarchy. It will go backward in time.

He tells me he has told Mr. Sevan many times that he would sacrifice anything, even himself, to bring peace to his country. He knows that the Afghan people want an end to war, but there are certain extremist elements that are against the UN peace plan. He is confident that eventually these elements will be isolated, and Afghanistan will emerge free and independent.

I tell him I hope the UN will be able to prevent any further bloodshed.

He speaks about his children, his wife. They are in New Delhi. He is eager to see them. [I think of my own children, and how much I miss them. But I am certain that I will see them again. What must it be like, I wonder, to fear that you will never again see your children?]

I say I think he is doing the right thing to remove himself from the political process. I hope others will appreciate his gesture.

He says that when he heard I'd arrived in Kabul, he felt good. It was a good sign. He had been waiting to meet me. He stands up and extends his hand to me. I stand up and shake his hand. He embraces me warmly.

[To the Afghan government, as well as to many other international actors in Kabul, my arrival signified that the United States was taking a more active interest in Afghanistan, and specifically, that it supported the UN plan for Afghanistan. The fact that the U.S. Ambassador to Pakistan had already stated his support for the UN plan was a matter of record. But there was still no U.S. Ambassador to Afghanistan, and the fact that a high ranking UN official, who was an American, had arrived in Kabul at this critical juncture was taken to signify an increased interest in Afghanistan on the part of the United States. It was pointless for me to say that I had come as a UN official, and not as a representative of my government. Which was the truth. The Afghans never would have believed it. I'm not even sure Benon and the rest of the UN staff would have believed it. It was simply assumed by members of the international community that every UN official, from whatever country, passed information to his government. Every man/woman in the UN was considered a spy, especially when involved in an event as strategic as war. And of course, some were. For my part, I never wasted my breath on spy talk. I let other people assume what they would.]

Avni comes out from the study where he has been with General Toukhi. He says it is time to leave for the airport. Toukhi will discuss the statement in the car with Najib. Najib has seen the statement earlier. There have not been major changes.

The Failed Escape of Najibullah

0145 hours. We load the baggage and begin a three-convoy movement to the airport. I am in the front car with Dan Quirke, a UN administrative officer and Irish national. We're in a four-wheel drive, Toyota Land Rover. Quirke is driving. Najib's bodyguard, with a [Soviet-made rifle known as a] Kalashnikov, is in the back seat with Najib's servant. The second car is a sedan. Avni is driving. Colonel Nowlan is sitting in front, and Najib and his brother are in back in that car. The third vehicle is a Toyota minibus, driven by Major Peter Beier, a UN blue beret from Denmark; with him are General Toukhi and his family.

We pass through several checkpoints, using the code word given to us by the minister of state security that afternoon. Benon has landed the UN plane at Kabul airport. He is inside the plane, waiting for us. [I doubt very much that he has brought with him the fifteen-member Council of Impartials. The original plan was to bring them to Kabul at the same time that Najib was leaving. That way, there would be a transfer of power with no break in the action. But the fact that Benon is arriving in the middle of the night suggests the plan has been abandoned. I have a bad feeling in my nervous stomach.]

When we come to the final checkpoint, we are halted. The guards will not let us pass. The password we have used for the first few checkpoints is suddenly invalid. Quirke tries the password several times, but the guards will not let us through. Then Quirke says a few words in the local language, hoping to convince the guards that everything has been agreed to, that it's all right. He keeps telling them everything is okay. But the guards will not budge. Quirke inches our vehicle forward as he talks. He has a jocular tone to his voice. It is as if he is trying to pull into a parking lot at the beach. Piece of cake. Let us through, he says.

But the guards will not budge. And they are annoyed that Quirke is inching forward. There are three or four of them. One raises his weapon to his shoulder. It is not easy to see them because it is the middle of the night, and the only light is from our headlights. The sky is overcast.

I implore Quirke to stop, to put on the brake. "They're not kidding," I say. "They'd just as soon shoot you as not."

Quirke is one of those fearless Irishmen I have met in peace-keeping operations all over the world. They push up against danger as if it were merely another hill to be climbed, as if all you needed were a little more effort. I was less daring. Quirke stops the car. "They're wearing different uniforms," he says.

"What do you mean?"

"They're wearing different uniforms than the guards at the other checkpoints."

"What does that mean?"

"It means they're special airport guards, or that the airport has changed hands."

"We've been double-crossed," I say.

"Probably," Quirke says.

Najib's bodyguard gets out of our car. He takes his Kalashnikov, but it is slung over his shoulder. He argues with the guards. He shouts at them. Colonel Nowlan gets out of his car, and comes to see what the trouble is. Avni gets out of his car. He wants to listen, not to argue. The shouting continues for about five minutes. I try to watch their gestures, but there is not very much light.

Meanwhile, Avni is in contact with Benon, who is on the UN plane at the airport. They are talking over the mobile phone. They are speaking in Turkish.

Avni comes over to tell us what is happening. The highest-ranking officer at the checkpoint is a sergeant. He has agreed to call his lieutenant to come to the checkpoint to talk to Najib's bodyguard. Dostom's Uzbek troops have seized the airport. They are not letting anyone through. Our password is useless. Perhaps one of the members of the executive committee of the Watan Party, with whom we made our agreement, is a follower of Kar-

mal, Najib's bitter rival and predecessor, and has leaked our plans
to Dostom. Or perhaps Dostom merely wants to take over now
that Najib has resigned, and he considers Najib to be his prisoner.
One should never underestimate the egomaniacal desire for power
among certain members of the human species. In any case, Dostom has seized the airport to prevent Najib's escape. He has sealed
it off. And apparently, government troops did not put up a fight.
As Colonel Nowlan told us recently, the defense perimeter of
Kabul is a joke. Dostom's troops will not allow anyone into the
airport for twenty-four hours. Meanwhile, Benon cannot disem-
bark. He has ordered the UN plane to be locked, so that no one
can board or leave. His plane is surrounded by troops.

A lieutenant arrives within ten minutes, and a bitter argument
ensues. There is a lot of shouting. Everyone is calling everyone else
names. This is not a negotiation. This is an exchange of threats and
insults. We sit and watch. After a while, the officer and Najib's
bodyguard go to speak to Najib. According to Avni, Najib is saying something like "Let us through, you asshole! Everything has
been arranged!" Najib has a booming voice, even from inside a car.
And he knows his life is at stake. After so many years in Afghanistan, after so many deaths behind him, he senses immediately what
his fate will be if he can't flee. Death has been his constant companion even his confidant, for the past decade, perhaps longer. But
the lieutenant claims he has no authority to let Najib through, and
that even if he could, our whole party would be slaughtered at the
airport, because Dostom's troops are not letting anyone in or out
of the airport for at least the next 24 hours. Once they have secured the airport, they will allow only certain flights to go in and
out. At this point, the Uzbeks will shoot anyone approaching the
airport, no questions asked, the lieutenant insists.

After several minutes of shouting, Najib makes a decision. He
has very little leverage, he has very few allies, and no longer any
power to intimidate or bribe. He tells Avni to turn around. He is
convinced they will not be able to reach the airport tonight. Avni
asks Najib if he wants to return to his residence. "No!" Najib
says. The same forces which have prevented him from leaving
Kabul will kill him if he returns to his residence. The only safe
place is the OSGAP compound. The UN has an obligation to
protect him, he insists.

[It was as if, at this very moment, on this very spot, a power
vacuum replaced what little central authority still existed in Af-

ghanistan; and that is why, I am convinced, this event must be given due significance in any history of this period. On this night, within a few hundred yards of Kabul airport, the sitting president of Afghanistan, Najibullah—a.k.a. Najib-e-Gao, or Najib the Bull—was deposed by anarchy. There had been varying degrees of anarchy in the country for months, but it had never triumphed until that night. Perhaps there would have been anarchy anyway, even if Najib had been able to board the UN plane. Or perhaps his official resignation and sudden exile might have pushed the factions meeting in Peshawar to reach an agreement on the Council of Impartials. We shall never know. But what we do know is that the gods of anarchy, which had been hovering over poor Afghanistan ever since the Soviet Union's withdrawal three years before, descended that night and took control. To be followed within a few years by a murderous medieval gang, swaddled in sanctimony and nurtured in Pakistan, known as the Taliban.]

THE HISTORY OF NATIONS
Chapter 4

The Taliban Era

The Rise of the Taliban

By Ahmed Rashid

When the Soviet army finally withdrew from Afghanistan in 1989, the Afghans who opposed the Communist leadership were jubilant. However, their joy did not last long. The Communist regime of Mohammad Najibullah managed to stay in power in Kabul for another three years. And in the countryside, some of the mujahideen warlords who had successfully fought the Soviets were doing everything they could to increase their own power and fortunes while abusing ordinary Afghans. Afghanistan, it seemed, had traded one brutal conqueror for another. Life was particularly harsh for citizens in the border areas, which attracted mujahideen rulers who wanted to make money smuggling drugs and contraband.

The situation infuriated a group of religious students, the boys and men who had left Afghanistan to study in madrassas, or religious schools, in neighboring Pakistan. This group of students, who called themselves the Taliban (a word that means "those who study the Koran" in the Persian and Pashto languages of Afghanistan), ultimately decided that they had to do something to end the corrupt activities in their homeland. In 1994 they fought with the mujahideen groups around the southern city of Kandahar and soon gained power there. They then laid siege to the capital city of Kabul, capturing it in 1996. The following selection by Ahmed Rashid describes how the Taliban subdued the mujahideen and seized power in Afghanistan. Ahmed Rashid reports on Afghanistan, Pakistan, and other areas of central Asia for the Far Eastern Economic Review, *an international journal.*

Afghanistan was in a state of virtual disintegration just before the Taliban emerged at the end of 1994. The country was divided into warlord fiefdoms and all the warlords had fought, switched sides and fought again in a bewildering array of alliances, betrayals and bloodshed. The predominantly [eth-

Ahmed Rashid, *Taliban: Militant Islam, Oil, and Fundamentalism in Central Asia.* New Haven, CT: Yale University Press, 2000. Copyright © 2000 by Ahmed Rashid. Reproduced by permission.

nic] Tajik government of President Burhanuddin Rabbani controlled Kabul, its environs and the north-east of the country, while
three provinces in the west centring on Herat were controlled by
Ismael Khan. In the east on the Pakistan border three [ethnic ma-
jority] Pashtun provinces were under the independent control of
a council or Shura (Council) of Mujaheddin commanders based
in Jalalabad. A small region to the south and east of Kabul was
controlled by [Mujaheddin warlord] Gulbuddin Hikmetyar.

In the north the Uzbek warlord General Rashid Dostum held
sway over six provinces and in January 1994 he had abandoned
his alliance with the Rabbani government and joined with Hikmetyar to attack Kabul. In central Afghanistan the Hazaras controlled the province of Bamiyan. Southern Afghanistan and Kandahar were divided up amongst dozens of petty ex-Mujaheddin
warlords and bandits who plundered the population at will. With
the tribal structure and the economy in tatters, no consensus on
a Pashtun leadership and Pakistan's unwillingness to provide military aid to the Durranis as they did to Hikmetyar, the Pashtuns
in the south were at war with each other.

International aid agencies were fearful of even working in
Kandahar as the city itself was divided by warring groups. Their
leaders sold off everything to Pakistani traders to make money,
stripping down telephone wires and poles, cutting trees, selling
off factories, machinery and even road rollers to scrap merchants.
The warlords seized homes and farms, threw out their occupants
and handed them over to their supporters. The commanders
abused the population at will, kidnapping young girls and boys
for their sexual pleasure, robbing merchants in the bazaars and
fighting and brawling in the streets. Instead of refugees returning from Pakistan, a fresh wave of refugees began to leave Kandahar for Quetta.

Intolerable Conditions

For the powerful mafia of truck transporters based in Quetta and
Kandahar, it was an intolerable situation for business. In 1995 I
travelled the short 130 miles by road from Quetta to Kandahar
and we were stopped by at least 20 different groups, who had put
chains across the road and demanded a toll for free passage. The
transport mafia who were trying to open up routes to smuggle
goods between Quetta and Iran and the newly independent state
of Turkmenistan, found it impossible to do business.

For those Mujaheddin who had fought the [1986–1992] Najibullah regime and had then gone home or to continue their
studies at *madrassas* in Quetta and Kandahar, the situation was particularly galling. 'We all knew each other—Mullahs [tribal lead-
ers] Omar, Ghaus, Mohammed Rabbani (no relation to President
Rabbani) and myself—because we were all originally from Urozgan province and had fought together,' said Mullah Hassan. 'I
moved back and forth from Quetta and attended *madrassas* there,
but whenever we got together we would discuss the terrible
plight of our people living under these bandits. We were people
of the same opinions and we got on with each other very well,
so it was easy to come to a decision to do something,' he added.

Mullah Mohammed Ghaus, the one-eyed Foreign Minister of
the Taliban, said much the same. 'We would sit for a long time to
discuss how to change the terrible situation. Before we started we
had only vague ideas what to do and we thought we would fail,
but we believed we were working with Allah as His pupils. We
have got so far because Allah has helped us,' said Ghaus.

Other groups of Mujaheddin in the south were also discussing
the same problems. 'Many people were searching for a solution.
I was from Kalat in Zabul province (85 miles north of Kandahar)
and had joined a *madrassa*, but the situation was so bad that we
were distracted from our studies and with a group of friends we
spent all our time discussing what we should do and what needed
to be done,' said Mullah Mohammed Abbas, who was to become
the Minister of Public Health in Kabul. 'The old Mujaheddin
leadership had utterly failed to bring peace. So I went with a
group of friends to Herat to attend the Shura called by Ismael
Khan, but it failed to come up with a solution and things were
getting worse. So we came to Kandahar to talk with Mullah
Omar and joined him,' Abbas added.

The Taliban's Goals

After much discussion these divergent but deeply concerned
groups chalked out an agenda which still remains the Taliban's
declared aims—restore peace, disarm the population, enforce
Sharia law and defend the integrity and Islamic character of Afghanistan. As most of them were part-time or full-time students
at *madrassas*, the name they chose for themselves was natural. A
talib is an Islamic student, one who seeks knowledge compared
to the mullah who is one who gives knowledge. By choosing

such a name the Taliban (plural of *Talib*) distanced themselves from the party politics of the Mujaheddin and signalled that they were a movement for cleansing society rather than a party trying to grab power.

All those who gathered around Omar were the children of the jihad but deeply disillusioned with the factionalism and criminal activities of the once idealised Mujaheddin leadership. They saw themselves as the cleansers and purifiers of a guerrilla war gone astray, a social system gone wrong and an Islamic way of life that had been compromised by corruption and excess. Many of them had been born in Pakistani refugee camps, educated in Pakistani *madrassas* and had learnt their fighting skills from Mujaheddin parties based in Pakistan. As such the younger Taliban barely knew their own country or history, but from their *madrassas* they learnt about the ideal Islamic society created by the Prophet Mohammed 1,400 years ago and this is what they wanted to emulate.

Some Taliban say Omar was chosen as their leader not for his political or military ability, but for his piety and his unswerving belief in Islam. Others say he was chosen by God. 'We selected Mullah Omar to lead this movement. He was the first amongst equals and we gave him the power to lead us and he has given us the power and authority to deal with people's problems,' said Mullah Hassan. Omar himself gave a simple explanation to Pakistani journalist Rahimullah Yousufzai. 'We took up arms to achieve the aims of the Afghan jihad and save our people from further suffering at the hands of the so-called Mujaheddin. We had complete faith in God Almighty. We never forgot that. He can bless us with victory or plunge us into defeat,' said Omar.

The Secrecy of Mullah Omar

No leader in the world today [in 2000] is surrounded by as much secrecy and mystery as Mullah Mohammed Omar.[1] Aged 39, he has never been photographed or met with Western diplomats and journalists. His first meeting with a UN diplomat was in October 1998, four years after the Taliban emerged, when he met with the UN Special Representative for Afghanistan Lakhdar Brahimi, because the Taliban were faced with a possibly devastating attack by Iran. Omar lives in Kandahar and has visited the capital Kabul

1. Omar has been in hiding since the U.S. invasion of Afghanistan in 2001. He is wanted by U.S. authorities for harboring al Qaeda head Osama bin Laden.

twice and only then very briefly. Putting together the bare facts of his life has become a full-time job for most Afghans and foreign diplomats.

Omar was born sometime around 1959 in Nodeh village near Kandahar to a family of poor, landless peasants who were members of the Hotak tribe, the Ghilzai branch of Pashtuns. The Hotaki chief Mir Wais, had captured [the city of] Isfahan in Iran in 1721 and established the first Ghilzai Afghan empire in Iran only to be quickly replaced by Ahmad Shah Durani. Omar's tribal and social status was non-existent and notables from Kandahar say they had never heard of his family. During the 1980s jihad his family moved to Tarinkot in Urozgan province—one of the most backward and inaccessible regions of the country where Soviet troops rarely penetrated. His father died while he was a young man and the task of fending for his mother and extended family fell upon him.

Looking for a job, he moved to Singesar village in the Mewand district of Kandahar province, where he became the village mullah and opened a small *madrassa*. His own studies in *madrassas* in Kandahar were interrupted twice, first by the Soviet invasion and then by the creation of the Taliban. Omar joined Khalis's Hizb-e-Islami [resistance group] and fought under commander Nek Mohammed against the [Mohammad] Najibullah regime between 1989 and 1992. He was wounded four times once in the right eye which is now permanently blinded.

Despite the success of the Taliban, Singesar is still like any other Pashtun village. Mud-brick homes plastered with more mud and straw are built behind high compound walls–a traditional defensive feature of Pashtun homes. Narrow, dusty alleyways, which turn into mud baths when it rains, connect village homes. Omar's *madrassa* is still functioning—a small mud hut with a dirt floor and mattresses strewn across it for the boys to sleep on. Omar has three wives, who continue living in the village and are heavily veiled. While his first and third wives are from Urozgan, his teenage second wife Guljana, whom he married in 1995, is from Singesar. He has a total of five children who are studying in his *madrassa*.

A tall, well-built man with a long, black beard and a black turban, Omar has a dry sense of humour and a sarcastic wit. He remains extremely shy of outsiders, particularly foreigners, but he is accessible to the Taliban. When the movement started he would offer his Friday prayers at the main mosque in Kandahar and mix with the people, but subsequently he has become much more of a recluse, rarely venturing outside Kandahar's administrative mansion where he lives. He now visits his village infrequently and when he does he is always accompanied by dozens of bodyguards in a convoy of deluxe Japanese jeepsters with darkened windows.

Omar speaks very little in Shura meetings, listening to other points of view. His shyness makes him a poor public speaker and despite the mythology that now surrounds him, he has little charismatic appeal. All day he conducts business from a small office in the mansion. At first he used to sit on the cement floor alongside visiting Taliban, but he now sits on a bed while others sit on the floor—a move that emphasises his status as leader. He has several secretaries who take notes from his conversations with commanders, ordinary soldiers, ulema [religious scholars] and plaintiffs and there is always the crackle of wireless sets as commanders around the country communicate with him.

Business consists of lengthy debate and discussions which end with the issuing of 'chits' or scraps of paper on which are written instructions allowing commanders to make an attack, ordering a Taliban governor to help out a plaintiff or a message to UN mediators. Formal communications to foreign embassies in Islamabad were frequently dictated by Pakistani advisers. . . .

The Taliban Are Mobilized

There is now an entire factory of myths and stories to explain how Omar mobilized a small group of Taliban against the rapacious Kandahar warlords. The most credible story, told repeatedly, is that in the spring of 1994 Singesar neighbours came to tell him that a commander had abducted two teenage girls, their heads had been shaved and they had been taken to a military camp and repeatedly raped. Omar enlisted some 30 *Talibs* who had only 16 rifles between them and attacked the base, freeing the girls and hanging the commander from the barrel of a tank. They captured quantities of arms and ammunition. 'We were fighting against Muslims who had gone wrong. How could we remain quiet when we could see crimes being committed against women and the poor?' Omar said later.

A few months later two commanders confronted each other in Kandahar, in a dispute over a young boy whom both men wanted to sodomise. In the fight that followed civilians were killed. Omar's group freed the boy and public appeals started coming in for the Taliban to help out in other local disputes. Omar had emerged as a Robin Hood figure, helping the poor against the rapacious commanders. His prestige grew because he asked for no reward or credit from those he helped, only demanding that they follow him to set up a just Islamic system.

At the same time Omar's emissaries were gauging the mood of other commanders. His colleagues visited Herat to meet with Ismael Khan [the leader of the province] and in September [1994] Mulla Mohammed Rabbani, a founding member of the Taliban, visited Kabul and held talks with President Rabbani. The isolated Kabul government wished to support any new Pashtun force that would oppose Hikmetyar, who was still shelling Kabul, and Rabbani promised to help the Taliban with funds if they opposed Hikmetyar.

However the Taliban's closest links were with Pakistan where many of them had grown up and studied in *madrassas* run by the mercurial Maulana Fazlur Rehman and his Jamiat-e-*Ulema* Islam (JUI), a fundamentalist party which had considerable support amongst the Pashtuns in Baluchistan and the North West Frontier Province (NWFP). More significantly Maulana Rehman was now a political ally of Prime Minister [of Pakistan] Benazir Bhutto and he had access to the government, the army and the ISI [Pakistan's intelligence agency Inter-Services Intelligence] to whom he described this newly emerging force. . . .

On 20 October 1994 [Interior Minister Naseerullah] Babar took a party of six Western ambassadors to Kandahar and Herat, without even informing the Kabul government. The delegation included senior officials from the departments of Railways, Highways, Telephones and Electricity. Babar said he wanted to raise US$300 million from international agencies to rebuild the highway from Quetta to Herat. On 28 October, Bhutto met with Ismael Khan and General Rashid Dostum in Ashkhabad and urged them to agree to open a southern route, where trucks would pay just a couple of tolls on the way and their security would be guaranteed.

However, before that meeting a major event had shaken the Kandahar warlords. On 12 October 1994 some 200 Taliban from Kandahar and Pakistani *madrassas* arrived at the small Afghan border post of Spin Baldak on the Pakistan-Afghanistan border just opposite Chaman. The grimy grease pit in the middle of the desert was an important trucking and fuelling stop for the transport mafia and was held by Hikmetyar's men. Here Afghan trucks picked up goods from Pakistani trucks, which were not allowed to cross into Afghanistan and fuel was smuggled in from Pakistan to feed the warlords' armies. For the transport mafia, control of the town was critical. They had already donated several hundred thousand Pakistani Rupees to Mullah Omar and promised a monthly stipend to the Taliban, if they would clear the roads of chains and bandits and guarantee the security for truck traffic.

The Taliban force divided into three groups and attacked Hikmetyar's garrison. After a short, sharp battle they fled, losing seven dead and several wounded. The Taliban lost only one man. Pakistan then helped the Taliban by allowing them to capture a large arms dump outside Spin Baldak that had been guarded by Hikmetyar's men. This dump had been moved across the border from Pakistan into Afghanistan in 1990, when the terms of the Geneva Accords obliged Islamabad not to hold weapons for Afghans on Pakistani territory. At the dump the Taliban seized some 18,000 kalashnikovs [rifles], dozens of artillery pieces, large quantities of ammunition and many vehicles.

The Fall of Kandahar

The capture of Spin Baldak worried the Kandahar warlords and they denounced Pakistan for backing the Taliban, but they continued bickering amongst themselves rather than uniting to meet the new threat. Babar was now getting impatient and he ordered a 30 truck test-convoy to travel to Ashkhabad with a load of medicines. 'I told Babar we should wait two months because we had no agreements with the Kandahar commanders, but Babar insisted on pushing the convoy through. The commanders suspected that the convoy was carrying arms for a future Pakistani force,' a Pakistani official based in Kandahar later told me.

On 29 October 1994, the convoy drawn from the army's National Logistics Cell (NLC), which had been set up in the 1980s by the ISI to funnel US arms to the Mujaheddin, left Quetta with 80 Pakistani ex-army drivers. Colonel Imam, the ISI's most prominent field officer operating in the south and Pakistan's Consul General in Herat, was also on board. Along with him were two young Taliban commanders, Mullahs Borjan and

[Nooruddin] Turabi. (Both were later to lead the Taliban's first assault on Kabul where Mullah Borjan was to meet his death.) Twelve miles outside Kandahar, at Takht-e-Pul near the perimeter of Kandahar airport, the convoy was held up by a group of commanders, Amir Lalai, Mansur Achakzai, who controlled the airport, and Ustad Halim. The convoy was ordered to park in a nearby village at the foot of low-lying mountains. When I walked the area a few months later the remains of camp fires and discarded rations were still evident.

The commanders demanded money, a share of the goods and that Pakistan stop supporting the Taliban. As the commanders negotiated with Colonel Imam, Islamabad imposed a news blackout for three days on the convoy hijack. 'We were worried that Mansur would put arms aboard the convoy and then blame Pakistan. So we considered all the military options to rescue the convoy, such as a raid by the Special Services Group (Pakistan army commandos) or a parachute drop. These options were considered too dangerous so we then asked the Taliban to free the convoy,' said a Pakistani official. On 3 November 1994, the Taliban moved in to attack those holding the convoy. The commanders, thinking this was a raid by the Pakistani army, fled. Mansur was chased into the desert by the Taliban, captured and shot dead with ten of his bodyguards. His body was hung from a tank barrel for all to see.

That same evening, the Taliban moved on Kandahar where, after two days of sporadic fighting they routed the commanders' forces. Mullah Naquib, the most prominent commander inside the city who commanded 2,500 men, did not resist. Some of his aides later claimed that Naquib had taken a substantial bribe from the ISI to surrender, with the promise that he would retain his command. The Taliban enlisted his men and retired the Mullah to his village outside Kandahar. The Taliban captured dozens of tanks, armoured cars, military vehicles, weapons and most significantly at the airport six Mig-21 fighters and six transport helicopters—left-overs from the Soviet occupation.

In just a couple of weeks this unknown force had captured the second largest city in Afghanistan with the loss of just a dozen men. In Islamabad no foreign diplomat or analyst doubted that they had received considerable support from Pakistan. The fall of Kandahar was celebrated by the Pakistan government and the JUI. Babar took credit for the Taliban's success, telling journalists privately that the Taliban were 'our boys'. Yet the Taliban demonstrated their independence from Pakistan, indicating that they were nobody's puppet. On 16 November 1994 Mullah Ghaus said that Pakistan should not bypass the Taliban in sending convoys in the future and should not cut deals with individual warlords. He also said the Taliban would not allow goods bound for Afghanistan to be carried by Pakistani trucks—a key demand of the transport mafia.

The Taliban cleared the chains from the roads, set up a one-toll system for trucks entering Afghanistan at Spin Baldak and patrolled the highway from Pakistan. The transport mafia was ecstatic and in December the first Pakistani convoy of 50 trucks carrying raw cotton from Turkmenistan arrived in Quetta, after paying the Taliban 200,000 rupees (US$5,000) in tolls. Meanwhile thousands of young Afghan Pashtuns studying in Baluchistan and the NWFP rushed to Kandahar to join the Taliban. They were soon followed by Pakistani volunteers from JUI *madrassas*, who were inspired by the new Islamic movement in Afghanistan. By December 1994, some 12,000 Afghan and Pakistani students had joined the Taliban in Kandahar. . . .

The Taliban immediately implemented the strictest interpretation of Sharia law ever seen in the Muslim world. They closed down girls' schools and banned women from working outside the home, smashed TV sets, forbade a whole array of sports and recreational activities and ordered all males to grow long beards. In the next three months the Taliban were to take control of 12 of Afghanistan's 31 provinces, opening the roads to traffic and disarming the population. As the Taliban marched north to Kabul, local warlords either fled or, waving white flags, surrendered to them. Mullah Omar and his army of students were on the march across Afghanistan.

Taliban Decrees Concerning Women and Behavior

By Amr Bil Maruf and Nai Az Munkar

Trained in the Islamic madrassas, or religious schools, in Pakistan, the Taliban leaders sought to impose sharia, or the laws of the Koran, when they seized control of Afghanistan in 1996. The regime applied Islamic law to every aspect of daily life, including public behavior and demeanor, the clothing women could wear, and the responsibilities of men to keep their families in line. To enforce these regulations, the Taliban established a religious police force to patrol the streets and punish infractions. In Kabul and other cities, beatings and public executions became commonplace events. In November 1996 the Taliban leaders Amr Bil Maruf and Nai Az Munkar published a set of decrees about women and cultural conduct, which is extracted in the following selection.

(This translation from Dari [one of the languages used in Afghanistan] was handed to Western agencies to implement; the grammar and spellings are reproduced here as they appeared in the original.)

Instructions for Women

Decree announced by the General Presidency of Amr Bil Maruf and Nai Az Munkar (Religious Police).

Kabul, November 1996.

Women you should not step outside your residence. If you go outside the house you should not be like women who used to go with fashionable clothes wearing much cosmetics and appear-

Amr Bil Maruf and Nai Az Munkar, Taliban decree relating to women and other issues, November/December 1996.

ing in front of every men before the coming of Islam.

Islam as a rescuing religion has determined specific dignity for women, Islam has valuable instructions for women. Women should not cream such opportunity to attract the attention of useless people who will not look at them with a good eye. Women have the responsibility as a teacher or coordinator for her family. Husband, brother, father have the responsibility for providing the family with the necessary life requirements (food, clothes etc.). In case women are required to go outside the residence for the purposes of education, social needs or social services they should cover themselves in accordance with Islamic Shari regulation. If women are going outside with fashionable, ornamental, right and charming clothes to show themselves, they will be cursed by the Islamic Sharia and should never expect to go to heaven.

All family elders and every Muslim have responsibility in this respect. We request all family elders to keep tight control over their families and avoid these problems. Otherwise these women will be threatened, investigated and severely punished as well as the family elders by the forces of the Religious Police (*Munkrat*).

The Religious Police have the responsibility and duty to struggle against these social problems and will continue their effort until evil is finished.

Rules for Hospitals and Clinics

Rules of work for the State Hospitals and private clinics based on Islamic Sharia principles. Ministry of Health, on behalf of Amir ul Momineen Mullah Mohammed Omar. Kabul, November 1996.

1. Female patients should go to female physicians. In case a male physician is needed, the female patient should be accompanied by her close relative.

2. During examination, the female patients and male physicians both should be dressed with Islamic *hijab* (veil).

3. Male physicians should not touch or see the other parts of female patients except for the affected part.

4. Waiting room for female patients should be safely covered.

5. The person who regulates turn for female patients should be a female.

6. During the night duty, in what rooms which female patients are hospitalized, the male doctor without the call of the patient is not allowed to enter the room.

7. Sitting and speaking between male and female doctors are not allowed, if there be need for discussion, it should be done with *hijab*.

8. Female doctors should wear simple clothes, they are not allowed to wear stylish clothes or use cosmetics or make-up.

9. Female doctors and nurses are not allowed to enter the rooms where male patients are hospitalized.

10. Hospital staff should pray in mosques on time.

11. The Religious Police are allowed to go for control at any time and nobody can prevent them.

Anybody who violates the order will be punished as per Islamic regulations.

Guidelines for Punishment

General Presidency of Amr Bil Maruf. Kabul, December 1996.

1. To prevent sedition and female uncovers (Be Hejabi). No drivers are allowed to pick up women who are using Iranian *burqa*. In case of violation the driver will be imprisoned. If such kind of female are observed in the street their house will be found and their husband punished. If the women use stimulating and attractive cloth and there is no accompany of close male relative with them, the drivers should not pick them up.

2. To prevent music. To be broadcasted by the public information resources. In shops, hotels, vehicles and rickshaws cassettes and music are prohibited. This matter should be monitored within five days. If any music cassette found in a shop, the shopkeeper should be imprisoned and the shop locked. If five people guarantee the shop should be opened the criminal released later. If cassette found in the vehicle, the vehicle and the driver will be imprisoned. If five people guarantee the vehicle will be released and the criminal released later.

3. To prevent beard shaving and its cutting. After one and a half months, if anyone observed has shaved and/or cut his beard, they should be arrested and imprisoned until their beard gets bushy.

4. To prevent keeping pigeons and playing with birds. Within ten days this habit/hobby should stop. After ten days this should be monitored and the pigeons and any other playing birds should be killed.

5. To prevent kite-flying. The kite shops in the city should be abolished.

6. To prevent idolatory. In vehicles, shops, hotels, room and any

other place pictures/portraits should be abolished. The monitors should tear up all pictures in the above places.

7. To prevent gambling. In collaboration with the security police the main centres should be found and the gamblers imprisoned for one month.

8. To eradicate the use of addiction. Addicts should be imprisoned and investigation made to find the supplier and the shop. The shop should be locked and the owner and user should be imprisoned and punished.

9. To prevent the British and American hairstyle. People with long hair should be arrested and taken to the Religious Police department to shave their hair. The criminal has to pay the barber.

10. To prevent interest on loans, charge on changing small denomination notes and charge on money orders. All money exchangers should be informed that the above three types of exchanging the money should be prohibited. In case of violation criminals will be imprisoned for a long time.

11. To prevent washing cloth by young ladies along the water streams in the city. Violator ladies should be picked up with respectful Islamic manner, taken to their houses and their husbands severely punished.

12. To prevent music and dances in wedding parties. In the case of violation the head of the family will be arrested and punished.

13. To prevent the playing of music drum. The prohibition of this should be announced. If anybody does this then the religious elders can decide about it.

14. To prevent sewing ladies cloth and taking female body measures by tailor. If women or fashion magazines are seen in the shop the tailor should be imprisoned.

15. To prevent sorcery. All the related books should be burnt and the magician should be imprisoned until his repentance.

16. To prevent not praying and order gathering pray at the bazaar. Prayer should be done on their due times in all districts. Transportation should be strictly prohibited and all people are obliged to go to the mosque. If young people are seen in the shops they will be immediately imprisoned.

The Northern Alliance Resists the Taliban

BY THE COUNCIL ON FOREIGN RELATIONS

When the Taliban captured Kandahar in 1994 and began to take control of Afghanistan, a group of northern tribal leaders banded together to fight it, forming the Northern Alliance. In 2001 when the United States led an invasion of Afghanistan to topple the Taliban regime that had supported the terrorist group al Qaeda, the Northern Alliance served as a U.S. ally and was able to take control of much of the country. The following selection from the Council on Foreign Relations describes the history of the Northern Alliance and how its members developed experience as mujahideen fighting the Soviet invasion of their country in 1979. The selection also explores the alliance's deplorable human rights record, states which countries supported and opposed the group, and briefly describes its leaders. The Council on Foreign Relations is an American foreign policy research organization. It publishes the journal Foreign Policy.

*W*hat is the Northern Alliance?

A loose confederation of Afghan militias and warlords drawn from Tajiks and other ethnic minorities living in the north of Afghanistan. The group ruled Afghanistan from 1992 to 1996, when the Taliban drove them from power. After the September 11 terrorist attacks [on New York City], the Northern Alliance—known formally as the National Islamic United Front for the Salvation of Afghanistan, or the United Front—joined the U.S.-led campaign to oust the Taliban and disrupt the al-Qaeda terrorist network.

Why did the United States pick the Northern Alliance as an ally?

Because the Northern Alliance provided a ground force that could fight the Taliban, which harbored al-Qaeda, the terrorist network that U.S. officials say was behind the September 11 attacks. As Defense Secretary Donald Rumsfeld put it, the Alliance "knew the lay of the land" and could "be a lot of help" in the U.S. campaign against al-Qaeda.

Do Northern Alliance members have a role in Afghanistan's government?

Yes. The Northern Alliance expected to take over Afghanistan after driving the Taliban from power, but pressure from the United States and Pakistan led to a power-sharing agreement with other Afghan opposition groups. More than half the posts in the U.N.-sponsored interim government created in December 2001 went to Alliance officials, including the foreign ministry, the interior ministry, and the ministry of defense. The Afghan government chosen by a June 2002 *loya jirga*, or grand council, also included many Alliance leaders, leading some members of Afghanistan's largest ethnic group, the Pashtuns, to complain that Tajiks from the Alliance are overrepresented in the new administration. The Afghan president, Hamid Karzai, was never a Northern Alliance member, although he did serve as deputy foreign minister under Northern Alliance rule in the early 1990s.

History

What is the history of the Northern Alliance?

Many Northern Alliance fighters got their start as *mujahedeen*, the Muslim fundamentalists who fought the 1979 Soviet invasion of Afghanistan. After the battered Soviets withdrew in 1989, the *mujahedeen* turned against Afghanistan's communist president, Muhammad Najibullah, and toppled him in 1992. The Northern Alliance ruled Afghanistan for the next four years, a period marred by civil war between the Northern Alliance and Pashtun warlords and infighting among Alliance factions.

In 1996, the Taliban swept to power, driving the Northern Alliance into a small corner of northwest Afghanistan, where they remained until U.S. bombing began in response to September 11. Since only three countries recognized the Taliban as Afghanistan's legitimate government, the Northern Alliance retained Afghanistan's U.N. seat until the formation of the December 2001 interim government.

Did the Northern Alliance represent all of Afghanistan's ethnic groups?

No. The Northern Alliance was composed mainly of Tajiks and Uzbeks, who together make up about 30 percent of Afghans. The Alliance did not include Pashtuns, Afghanistan's largest ethnic group, with more than 40 percent of the population. This exclusion bred resentment during Northern Alliance rule and fed Pakistan's dislike for the Alliance. Moreover, the Northern Alliance once persecuted Hazaras, who comprise 20 percent of the population, and expelled them from the Afghan capital of Kabul in 1995. In later years, however, the Alliance also contained Hazara factions.

Which foreign countries supported the Northern Alliance?

Before September 2001, the Alliance had close ties with neighboring Tajikistan and was also backed by Uzbekistan, India, Russia, Iran, Turkey, Kazakhstan, and Kyrgyzstan. After the September 11 attacks, the United States lent material and logistical support to the Northern Alliance—a decisive factor in the fall of the Taliban.

What foreign countries opposed the Northern Alliance?

Pakistan. Pakistan's substantial Pashtun minority supported their Taliban brethren across the border, and the government, wary of Pashtun separatism, lent its support. In addition to ethnic ties, Pakistan wanted a friendly state on its western border to balance India, its great rival to the east. Once the group's staunchest foreign supporter, Pakistan dropped the Taliban after September 11 but urged the United States to restrain the Northern Alliance when they took Kabul in November 2001.

Who led the Northern Alliance?

Officially, the Northern Alliance was led by Burhanuddin Rabbani, an Islamic scholar and poet who became Afghanistan's president in 1992 and was dislodged by the Taliban in 1996. The Alliance's most visible and charismatic figure, however, was its late defense minister, Ahmed Shah Masoud, known as the "Lion of Panjshir." A legendary *mujahedeen* commander and a brilliant tactician, Masoud had pledged to bring freedom and democracy to Afghanistan. He was assassinated on September 9, 2001, by two men claiming to be Moroccan journalists. His killers are thought to have been agents of al-Qaeda acting in concert with the September 11 plot.

How was the Northern Alliance's human rights record during its time in power?

"Deplorable," according to Human Rights Watch. There was "virtually no rule of law" in areas controlled by the Alliance, and Alliance members were guilty of summary executions, arbitrary arrest, torture, and forced "disappearances." The ongoing civil war made life even more miserable. In 1994 and 1995, battles between Northern Alliance factions for control of Kabul killed some 12,000 civilians and reduced the capital, which had largely escaped damage during the ten-year war with the Soviets, to rubble. As a result of this misrule, many Afghans welcomed the Taliban when they entered Kabul in 1996, promising to restore law and order.

Did the Alliance improve its record while it was out of power?

Not really. According to Human Rights Watch, the Northern Alliance committed numerous massacres in their war against the Taliban; in 1997, for example, when Alliance troops captured the important northern city of Mazar-i-Sharif, they killed at least 3,000 Taliban captives, throwing some down wells and blowing up others with hand grenades. Human rights organizations reported that, after the Taliban fell, Northern Alliance warlords loaded enemy prisoners into freight containers and dumped their bodies in mass graves.

Did the Northern Alliance treat women any better than the Taliban?

Somewhat. In areas of Afghanistan under Northern Alliance command, girls were allowed to go to school, and women weren't forced to wear the *burka*, a full-body covering. But most women veiled themselves anyway, and some experts warn that the Northern Alliance has pressured them to do so. Furthermore, Alliance troops allegedly harassed women and committed widespread rape in Kabul in 1995. According to Taliban lore, Mullah Muhammad Omar founded the group to prevent the Northern Alliance's abuse of women.

Was the Northern Alliance involved with the drug trade?

Yes. Opium poppies are Afghanistan's most profitable crop, and, according to the State Department, the Alliance did little to stop the cultivation and smuggling of opium in the territory it controlled. U.S. officials allege that some warlords affiliated with the Northern Alliance are "deeply involved" with the drug trade and may have used drug money to fund their operations.

The U.S.-Led Attack on the Taliban

By Stephen Tanner

Soon after the September 11, 2001, terrorist attacks on the World Trade Center and the Pentagon, U.S. and British intelligence agents discovered that the men responsible for the attacks were connected to the al Qaeda terrorist network run by Osama bin Laden, who was in Afghanistan. The United States demanded that the Taliban government of Afghanistan surrender Bin Laden to U.S. officials. When the Taliban refused, a U.S.-led coalition mounted an attack on Afghanistan that overthrew the Taliban and disrupted the operations of al Qaeda. In this selection Stephen Tanner traces the major events of the 2001 U.S.-led war against the Taliban. Tanner argues that the United States was able to achieve victory relatively quickly because the Afghans themselves were eager to overthrow the Taliban regime. Stephen Tanner is a military historian and freelance writer. He is the author of Afghanistan: A Military History from Alexander the Great to the Fall of the Taliban.

[A fter the September 11, 2001, attacks on the World Trade Center and the Pentagon] it only took a day for U.S. intelligence to identify many of the September 11 terrorists, provide headshots, their recent movements, and to confirm their connection to Osama Bin Laden's Al Qaeda organization. The flurry of communications intercepts and data tracked by the CIA, FBI, and NSA [National Security Agency] prior to the attack had revealed that something was about to happen; they just hadn't known what, where, or how big. It was only after the attacks that all the pieces came together over the remains of nineteen suicidal Arab hijackers, fifteen of them from Saudi

Stephen Tanner, *Afghanistan: A Military History from Alexander the Great to the Fall of the Taliban.* New York: Da Capo Press, 2002. Copyright © 2002 by Stephen Tanner. Reproduced by permission of Da Capo, a member of Perseus Books LLC.

Arabia, who from different locations on the East Coast had co-ordinated the four separate operations.

Congress appropriated $40 billion for antiterror operations, though in fact, [President George W.] Bush received an open checkbook on the fourteenth when the Senate voted unani-mously to authorize "all necessary and appropriate force." The president then laid down the gauntlet to the world at large: "You're either with us or against us." He sought to create a greater coalition of nations in support of the U.S. response to September 11 than his father had assembled for the Gulf War in 1990.

The first step was to demand that the Taliban government in Afghanistan hand over Osama Bin Laden. [Taliban leader] Mul-lah Omar instinctively refused. A delegation from Pakistan, headed by ISI [Pakistan's intelligence organization] general Faiz Gilani, traveled to Kandahar to convince Omar to give up Bin Laden and his Al Qaeda associates. The Taliban attempted to bar-gain, demanding diplomatic recognition, cessation of foreign sup-port for the Northern Alliance, and a resumption of foreign aid. Omar also demanded "convincing evidence" of Bin Laden's in-volvement. At this time an odd dynamic occurred in the Islamic world, wherein a majority of people claimed to believe in Bin Laden's innocence, even while his photo was paraded at demon-strations and displayed as large posters in families' living rooms. He had become an outlaw superstar to much of the Islamic world, a status reinforced rather than dimmed by America's re-solve to get him, in Bush's words, "dead or alive."

The World Reacts

World reaction to the September 11 attacks was a combination of deep sympathy for the loss of so many innocents, fear of some kind of berserk American response, and pragmatic interest now that the U.S. was fully engaged against Islamic radicals. Israeli Prime Minister Ariel Sharon canceled peace talks he had sched-uled with Yasser Arafat of the Palestinian Authority on the the-ory that after September 11 U.S. pressure to compromise with the Arabs would disappear. Russia offered its support to the United States while anticipating its own battles against Islamic extremists in Chechnya would no longer be criticized. India stiff-ened its back against the Muslim terrorists who had been wag-ing war in Kashmir. [The Central Asian republic of] Uzbekistan, Tajikistan, and Kyrgyzstan welcomed U.S. emissaries requesting

base facilities, pleased to receive aid in return and a new power
in the region to balance the looming presence of Russia.

The country in the most ticklish position was Pakistan, which
had all but created the Taliban and had continued to support it
until September 11. (Pakistani shipments through Jalalabad continued into October, though were said to be the final remnants
of previous commitments.) General Pervez Musharraf, who had
taken power in a coup in 1999 now abandoned the Taliban and
offered the U.S. his full support. Pakistan had been shunned by
the U.S. since test-firing a nuclear bomb in 1994 and now saw
an opportunity to regain an ally, especially, if need be, for its continuing struggle against India. Musharraf had also been appalled
at the September 11 attacks and had found that the Taliban, like
a Frankenstein monster, had been slipping out of his control.

On September 20, 2001 President Bush addressed the U.S.
Congress and public with an eloquent, determined call to arms.
Many observers noted that the president, formerly known for
jocularity and tonguetied non sequiturs, now seemed transformed, with a steely gaze and unmistakable resolve. "The Taliban," he said, "must act and act immediately." His widely lauded
speech concluded:

> The course of this conflict is not known yet its out-
> come is certain. Freedom and fear, justice and cruelty,
> have always been at war. And we know that God is not
> neutral between them. . . . We'll meet violence with pa-
> tient justice, assured of the rightness of our cause and
> confident of the victories to come. In all that lies be-
> fore us, may God grant us wisdom and may he watch
> over the United States of America.

Operation Enduring Freedom

The Taliban mullahs responded with a call for holy war "if infidels invade an Islamic country." During the next two weeks,
American forces moved into place while fuel and munitions were
stockpiled at airbases from Spain to the Indian Ocean. Acting
upon reports of famine, and anxious not to antagonize the
broader world of Islam, the United States organized a massive
food lift into Afghanistan, dropping crates of packaged meals.
The code name for the forthcoming military campaign, "Infinite
Justice," was canceled after critics pointed out its religious over-

tone, as if Jehovah was about to come after Allah. Administration officials had already been advised not to use the word "crusade." The code name for the U.S. military effort was changed on September 25 to "Enduring Freedom."

Early in October, the U.S. revealed to a council of NATO nations the results of its investigations into the September 11 attacks. Proof of Al Qaeda responsibility was irrefutable. British Prime Minister Tony Blair was foremost among champions of the American cause. "This is a battle with only one outcome," he declared. "Our victory, not theirs." On October 6, Bush announced that "Full warning has been given, and time is running out."

The next day, October 7, American and British forces attacked Afghanistan. Fifteen land-based bombers and twenty-five carrier-based fighter bombers soared over the Hindu Kush [Mountains of Afghanistan] while fifty Tomahawk missiles were launched from U.S. ships and British submarines in the Arabian Sea. Targeted were Taliban compounds, command centers, and airfields. In the first hours, the small Taliban air force was destroyed on the ground, as was its supply of SA-2 and SA-3 antiaircraft missiles.

As the smoke cleared, an anonymous messenger dropped a package at the door of the Kabul bureau of Al Jazeera, an Arab television network based in Qatar. Inside was a videotaped speech from Osama Bin Laden. Dressed in camouflage and standing before a rock face with a rifle at his side, he began: "Here is America struck by God Almighty in one of its vital organs, so that its greatest buildings are destroyed." He went on to speak of eighty years of Islamic humiliation, starving Iraqi children, Israeli tanks in Palestine, and U.S. atomic attacks on Japan. He concluded his speech by renewing his call for global jihad:

> The wind of change is blowing to remove evil from the peninsula of Muhammed, peace be upon him. As to America, I say to it and its people a few words: I swear to God that America will not live in peace before peace reigns in Palestine, and before all the army of infidels depart the land of Muhammed, peace be upon him. God is the greatest and glory be to Islam.

U.S. airstrikes continued with B-1s flying from Diego Garcia, and huge, exotic B-2 stealth bombers crossing half the world at high subsonic speed from Whiteman Air Force Base, Missouri. Navy F-14s and F-18s flying from the *Enterprise* and *Carl Vinson* helped to obliterate seven Taliban compounds, though they appeared to have been hastily evacuated. AC-130 Spectre gunships arrived in the theater. These low-flying propellor aircraft bristled with 25mm Gatling guns and 40mm and 105mm cannon, all computer coordinated to focus on a ground target while the plane circled above it.

The airstrikes quickly became controversial as a United Nations compound in Kabul was accidentally hit, killing four workers; and, according to Taliban reports, dozens of civilians were killed in a village called Karam. On that same day, another errant 2,000-pound bomb hit a residence in the capital, decimating a family. Abdul Haq, a famous former mujahideen leader who had operated against the Soviets around Kabul, said that the bombing was counterproductive in that it would only rally Afghans around the Taliban. Part of the problem was that the United States soon became short of visible military targets. Pakistan's President Musharraf had insisted that the Americans not bomb Taliban troop positions facing the Northern Alliance near Kabul for fear that another Tajik-Uzbek takeover of the capital would only duplicate the 1992 situation that had resulted in a civil war with the Pashtuns. . . .

The Battle at the Front Lines

On October 21, U.S. warplanes began to pound Taliban frontline positions north of Kabul. Until then, Taliban soldiers had actually gone to the front for safety since the Americans were bombing everywhere else but there. Northern Alliance troops who had fought for years without air support now thrilled to the sight of history's strongest air force coming to their aid. The Americans employed 5,000-pound laser-guided "bunker busters" as well as 2,000-pound "smart bombs" (Joint Direct Attack Munitions, or JDAMs) guided by lasers or satellites. [U.S. secretary of defense Donald] Rumsfeld announced—more for Pakistani than American ears—why the U.S. had switched its effort to the front lines instead of persisting in attacks on the practically nonexistent Taliban infrastructure in the south. "It happens" he said, "that they are arrayed against, for the most part, Northern Alliance forces north of Kabul and in the northwest portion of the country." The Northern Alliance pitched in with rocket, artillery, and tank fire, answered in kind by the Taliban. Heavy machine-gun fire was exchanged by both sides across the rugged ridge lines and valleys. . . .

After a month of the U.S. bombing campaign, rumblings began to reach Washington from Europe, the Mideast, and Pakistan, from where Musharraf had requested that the bombing cease. Having begun the war with the greatest imaginable reservoir of moral authority, the U.S. was on the verge of letting it slip away through high-level attacks using the most ghastly inventions its scientists could come up with. Meanwhile, Taliban troops manned clear front lines, occasionally jeering at their Northern Alliance counterparts, while fifty thousand American forces in the theater (half naval) plus some two million in reserve in the U.S. and around the world seemed reluctant to engage.

Many Countries Pledge to Help the United States

On November 10 President Bush went to New York, where the wreckage of the World Trade Center still smoldered with underground fires, to address the United Nations. "Every nation has a stake in this cause," he reminded the assembled delegates. "As we meet, the terrorists are planning more murder, perhaps in my country, perhaps in yours." His words had impact. Most of the world renewed its support for the American effort, including commitments of material help from Germany, France, Italy, Japan, and other countries. To that point the United States and Britain, along with Canada and Australia, had been most active in the battle. One problem that prevented the international community from showing a more solid military front was that American air- and sea-lift capacity, its air and naval power, and existing base network were far superior to those of its allies. When European troops eventually arrived in Kabul, they disembarked from Ukrainian commercial airliners. In the Pentagon the realization set in that U.S. forces could act faster and more decisively without having to coordinate with a broad coalition of inferior military establishments.

But as winter approached, U.S. military planners anticipated that operations, including air strikes, would become more difficult. There was also a debate whether to pause during the Muslim holy month of Ramadan, due to begin in mid-November. The food airlift had petered out amid Taliban accusations that the packaged meals were poisoned and U.S. counterwarnings that the Taliban might poison them just to prove their point. The propaganda rationale for the food drops had in any case disappeared

MULLAH OMAR DEFENDS
A FATEFUL DECISION

In this short interview, broadcast on the Voice of America radio net-work, Mullah Mohammad Omar, a leader of the Taliban who is now in hiding, defends his refusal to turn over Osama bin Laden to the United States after the terrorist attacks of September 2001. The interview was pulled after senior U.S. Department of State and National Security Council officials publicly objected to it.

Voice of America interviewer: Why don't you expel Osama bin Laden?

Omar: This is not an issue of Osama bin Laden. It is an issue of Islam. Islam's prestige is at stake. So is Afghanistan's tradition.

VOA: Do you know that the US has announced a war on terrorism?

Omar: I am considering two promises. One is the promise of God, the other is that of [President George W.] Bush. The promise of God is that my land is vast. If you start a journey on God's path, you can reside anywhere on this earth and will be protected. . . . The promise of Bush is that there is no place on earth where you can hide that I cannot find you. We will see which one of these two promises is fulfilled.

VOA: But aren't you afraid for the people, yourself, the Taliban, your country?

Omar: Almighty God . . . is helping the believers and the Muslims. God says he will never be satisfied with the infidels. In terms of worldly affairs, America is very strong. Even if it were twice as strong or twice that, it could not be strong enough to defeat us. We are confident that no one can harm us if God is with us.

VOA: You are telling me you are not concerned, but Afghans all over the world are concerned.

Omar: We are also concerned. Great issues lie ahead. But we depend on God's mercy. Consider our point of view: if we give Osama away today, Muslims who are now pleading to give him up would then be reviling us for giving him up. ... Everyone is afraid of America and wants to please it. But Americans will not be able to prevent such acts like the one that has just occurred because America has taken Islam hostage. If you look at Islamic countries, the people are in despair. They are complaining that Islam is gone. But people remain firm in their Islamic beliefs. In their pain and frustration, some of them commit suicide acts. They feel they have nothing to lose.

VOA: What do you mean by saying America has taken the Islamic world hostage?

Omar: America controls the governments of the Islamic countries. The people ask to follow Islam, but the governments do not listen because they are in the grip of the United States. If someone follows the path of Islam, the government arrests him, tortures him or kills him. This is the doing of America. If it stops supporting those governments and lets the people deal with them, then such things won't happen. America has created the evil that is attacking it. The evil will not disappear even if I die and Osama dies and others die. The US should step back and review its policy. It should stop trying to impose its empire on the rest of the world, especially on Islamic countries.

VOA: So you won't give Osama bin Laden up?

Omar: No. We cannot do that. If we did, it means we are not Muslims ... that Islam is finished. If we were afraid of attack, we could have surrendered him the last time we were threatened and attacked. So America can hit us again, and this time we don't even have a friend.

VOA: If you fight America with all your might—can the Taliban do that? Won't America beat you and won't your people suffer even more?

Omar: I'm very confident that it won't turn out this way. Please note this: there is nothing more we can do except depend on almighty God. If a person does, then he is assured that the Almighty will help him, have mercy on him and he will succeed.

Mullah Omar, interviewed by Voice of America, 2001.

since Pakistani Pashtuns had not risen en masse in support of their Taliban cousins across the border. The Bush administration repeatedly warned the U.S. public to prepare for a long, hard war. Its estimate, however, was mistaken.

The Taliban Begins to Flee

By early November 2001, the Tajik mujahideen leader, Ismail Khan, had returned to his old stomping grounds in the west around Herat, and the Uzbek warlord Abdul Rashid Dostum had reorganized his loyal former troops in the north. Haji Mohaqiq mobilized fighters from the Hazarajat [the domain of the Hazaras descendants of the Mongols] within the Hindu Kush, where the Taliban, like the Soviets before them, had been largely reluctant to go. While Bush had been making his plaintive appeal before the United Nations, General Osta Atta Muhammad of the Northern Alliance had moved on the northern Afghan city of Mazar-i-Sharif from the east, cooperating with Dostum, who had placed his forces to the south. They overran the airport and then took Mazar after fighting for half an hour. The Taliban defenders defected or surrendered. Those who fled west were met by Ismail Khan, leading his forces to the scene northward from Herat. Many Taliban eagerly accepted Uzbek or Tajik protection against the Mongol-featured Hazaras, who remembered the Taliban slaughter of six thousand of their kinsmen in 1997.

In the northeast, Northern Alliance forces moved against the Taliban-held cities of Taliqan and Kunduz. Taliqan came under siege while Tajik commanders advised the Taliban leaders inside to surrender. One Taliban general, Abdullah Gard, went over to his Tajik opponent, Daoud Khan, with at least one thousand men. On November 11 the city fell without bloodshed, the remaining Pashtun defenders simply defecting to their longtime enemies. Northern Alliance troops rushing toward Taliban trenchlines north of Taliqan, however, were knocked back by a torrent of fire. Many Taliban in the north were foreign volunteers, more fanatic than the Pashtun and not so welcomed by Afghans if they surrendered. U.S. aircraft carefully roamed the skies, seeking targets of opportunity or responding to calls from Special Forces or USAF spotters on the ground.

British Special Air Service (SAS) commandos were also in Afghanistan. In one action reported by the London *Times* and the *Telegraph*, a "Sabre" team of about sixty men stormed a tunnel holding an equivalent number of Taliban fighters inside. The tally was two wounded SAS at the entrance and two more wounded in the subterranean gunfight, against eighteen dead Taliban and over forty captured. . . .

The Northern Alliance Enters Kabul

The Northern Alliance made rapid progress across the Shomali plain leading to Kabul. Taliban lines had been abandoned, some men retreating, others defecting and many making off for their homes. The city of Herat succumbed to Ismail Khan's men that afternoon, after six thousand Taliban had defected to the ex-mujahideen commander. Simultaneously, Kabul was officially abandoned by the Taliban, the remaining troops urged on by a message from Mullah Omar: "Take to the mountains. Defending the cities with front lines that can be targeted from the air will cause us terrible loss." Taliban columns retreating south of the city were hit by U.S. fighter bombers.

The Northern Alliance had promised the United States (representing Pakistan's worries) to halt two miles north of Kabul rather than enter the city and attempt to set up a new government. "We will encourage our friends to head south," said Bush, "but not into the city of Kabul itself." But after five years of battling the Taliban, the temptation to enter the capital was too great to ignore. On November 13, Northern Alliance troops marched into Kabul to the jubilation of many of its citizens. Though fears of urban fighting or large-scale atrocities were not realized, there were some ugly incidents. Several Taliban stragglers were humiliated, beaten, or executed. In one incident, six Arab and Pakistani Taliban sprung an ambush, two firing from up in the branches of a tree. After Northern Alliance troops killed them, their bodies were gleefully mutilated by citizens of Kabul, venting years of frustration.

The general scene was less gruesome. The harsh theocracy of Taliban rule had never sat well in Kabul, a city which had received a taste of modernization during the Soviet occupation and had always stood apart from the strict fundamentalism of the Afghan countryside. By way of greeting the Northern Alliance's arrival, music blared in the streets for the first time in years, and flowers were strewn in the path of tanks. Some women even took off their veils, though this was considered risky in case the Taliban suddenly returned, and because their liberators, as some women quickly remembered, were not Western troops but those who had formerly called themselves "soldiers of God."

Jalalabad was abandoned by the Taliban at the same time as Kabul, and Yunis Khalis, leader of one of the former Peshawar-based parties of mujahideen, quickly claimed control. Ismail Khan reorganized Herat while Dostum flew his flag again over Mazar-i-Sharif. Rumors abounded that Gulbuddin Hekmatyar would return from exile in Iran to reclaim his eastern Ghilzai territory south of Kabul. Aside from the lamented Massoud, all the major players of the Soviet war and the mujahideen civil war were reassuming their positions. Presidents Bush and Musharraf had meanwhile urgently complained to Rabbani, political head of the Northern Alliance, about his troops breaking their promise not to enter Kabul. Rabbani stated that his men were only there for security reasons and that only three thousand would remain in the capital.

A Pocket of Taliban Resistance

The northern half of Afghanistan had been cleared of Taliban except for the city of Kunduz, thirty-five miles west of Taliqan. There, remaining units of Pashtun Taliban congregated with diehard foreign volunteers and elements of Osama Bin Laden's Al Qaeda. The Northern Alliance surrounded the city and sent in congenial offers to surrender. On November 13, Tajik troops approached to accept the defection of an Afghan Pashtun contingent, but were suddenly fired upon by foreign volunteers who had learned of the plan. The Northern Alliance men scrambled back to their trenches after suffering several casualties. Present in Kunduz were scores of Arabs as well as Punjabis, Chinese, Chechens, and Indonesians, plus hundreds of Pakistanis and a scattering of other nationals who had signed on to the Taliban's cause.

Amid warnings from journalists such as [David] Rohde of the *New York Times* who wrote, "the country's political map is beginning to look ominously like the map of 1989," America and Britain rushed in elite troops, eight C-130s delivering 160 Green Berets and Royal Marines to Bagram air base north of Kabul on November 15. The problem was that the Taliban, for all its flaws, had actually established order in a country that had completely lacked it in the post-Soviet years when warlords vied for power. If the Taliban collapsed it was now incumbent on the Americans and their British allies not to allow the same situation to resume.

Suspicion that the Taliban had disappeared before they could truly be defeated was reinforced on November 19, when four

Western journalists were shot in cold blood on the mountainous road to Kabul from Jalalabad. According to a surviving witness, a gunman had said, "What did you think? It's the end of the Taliban? The Taliban are still here." The Tajik political leader Rabbani, meanwhile, assured the U.S. that he would not try to form a government, pending the decision of a council of Afghan leaders America had assembled in Bonn, Germany.

After the Taliban abandoned Kabul, some Americans became giddy about the easy victory. Afghanistan made it three straight wars—after Bosnia and Kosovo—in which U.S. troops had participated without suffering a single combat fatality. It seemed that the United States had stumbled onto a new form of warfare, perhaps one perfectly tailored for the twenty-first century. It involved devastating U.S. air power combined with a few specialists on the ground and "proxy" troops who would do the actual fighting. U.S. military casualties were thus unnecessary. With America now fully engaged in southern Asia, hawks were clamoring to expand the war by next attacking Iraq. Though Iraq had not been involved in the September 11 attacks, many in the Bush administration still held a grudge against Saddam Hussein for surviving the Gulf War and because of evidence he was building weapons of mass destruction. [President Bill] Clinton's former adviser, Dick Morris, was prominent among those advocating that the U.S. repeat its new formula of warfare by using Shi'ites in the south and Kurds in the north of Iraq as proxy troops in the next round.

Other Americans were displeased that Northern Alliance rather than U.S. soldiers were achieving the ground victory in Afghanistan. Though it was clear that Afghanistan was not a proper environment for heavy armor, many wondered what had become of legendary American formations such as the U.S. Marines, the 82nd and 101st Airborne Divisions, the 10th Mountain Division, or light elements of the 1st Infantry Division, the "Big Red One"? If September 11 had not provided the U.S. Army and Marines impetus enough to fight, what contingency would?

The Fall of Kunduz

The situation around Kunduz had meanwhile turned messy. It was apparent that many of the Taliban wanted to surrender, but Arabs and other diehard foreign volunteers were preventing them. Rumors came in that Arabs were shooting Taliban Pash-

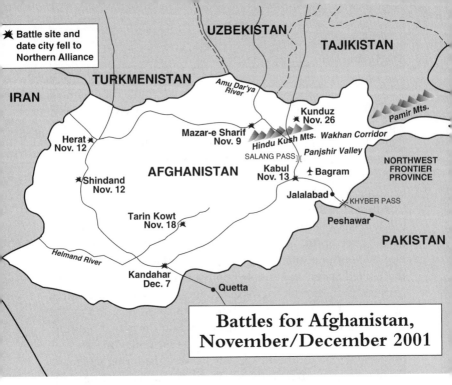

Battles for Afghanistan, November/December 2001

tuns in the city to prevent them from defecting. U.S. B-52s and fighter bombers plastered Taliban positions in and around the town. During the two-week siege, Northern Alliance troops reported a stream of Pakistani aircraft flying into Kunduz's airfield at night, taking their nationals to safety. Convoys of pickup trucks packed with Taliban meanwhile flowed south from Kunduz, Northern Alliance troops chasing them with occasional fire while basically letting them go. On November 24, Western journalists recorded the astonishing scene of about seven hundred Afghan Taliban emerging from the city waving and smiling in response to Northern Alliance cheers, even shaking hands with their besiegers. In contrast, some four hundred non-Afghan fighters—mostly Pakistani but including Arabs and others—were taken prisoner by Dostum and placed in a large nineteenth-century fortress called Qala Jangi near Mazar.

Kunduz fell on the twenty-sixth as Dostum's Uzbek troops roamed the streets killing last-ditch holdouts. . . .

Toward a New Government

In early December, the council of Afghan leaders in Bonn agreed to name Hamid Karzai, a Durrani Pashtun, head of an interim government. Rabbani, the political head of the Northern Alliance, stood aside, though with a profound silence that bordered on ominous. The interim government was nevertheless packed with Tajiks and other Northern Alliance representatives as heads of defense, intelligence, interior, and other important posts. . . .

While the U.S. pondered the problem of forming a proxy "Southern Alliance" that could match the achievements of the Northern one, Kandahar was abandoned by the Taliban on December 7. The Taliban capital thus fell exactly two months after American air strikes had begun and before any U.S. ground troops could get started. The city fell to two quarreling factions of Pashtuns who fired at each other in the process. Two days later, the last vestige of Taliban rule in Afghanistan disappeared when the province of Zabul, on the Pakistani border, surrendered.

The sudden collapse of the Taliban came as a surprise. It appeared, in fact, that for several years the Taliban regime had successfully concealed from the entire world its true fragility. The fierce rhetoric and fiery dedication of its leaders had disguised the fact that it sat on shaky ground, having instituted not only a politically autocratic but restrictive theocratic regime upon a country that was not accustomed to government rule at all. The withdrawal of Pakistani support was a major factor in its demise, as was the arrival of U.S. air power, blasting Taliban troops, installations, and convoys wherever they could be found. But the movement was primarily overthrown by the Afghans themselves. At one point the Taliban had been welcomed as a surprising solution that retrieved the country from anarchy, but its notion of order was not followed by skill at government. By 2001 most Afghans had become tired of the fanaticism, and when the country became the focus of the entire world's attention after September 11, the native population espied possible new hopes for the future.

The History of Nations

Chapter 5

The Current
Challenges

The Obstacles to Democratic Government

By Gordon Peake

In 2001 the United States overthrew Afghanistan's Taliban government. The Americans were helped by the Northern Alliance, a loose confederation of Afghan militias and warlords. Many members of the Northern Alliance thought that they would now rule Afghanistan, but the United States and the United Nations had different plans. Knowing that something had to be done to prevent Afghanistan from returning to the chaos and civil war that the country had suffered before the Taliban took over in 1996, world leaders were determined that a new, centralized government that was truly representative of the people should be formed.

A meeting in Bonn, Germany, in December 2001 established an interim government. Under pressure from the United States, Hamid Karzai was appointed temporary chairman, and a loya jirga (grand council) elected him interim president in June 2002. Under Karzai's leadership, the people prepared for a general election in 2004. From the outset, however, the proponents of a centralized, democratic government faced major problems, particularly from the Northern Alliance leaders who wanted power for themselves. Nevertheless, on October 9, 2004, Afghanistan held its first direct election ever, and Karzai was elected president with 55.4 percent of the votes.

The following selection describes the challenges Afghanistan faces as it attempts to create a centralized, democratic government. The most difficult problem is the weakness of the interim government, which does not have the strength to rein in warlords using private militias and violence to enforce their authority. Gordon Peake suggests that the international community will play a vital role in strengthening Afghanistan's new government and preventing local leaders from creating chaos in the country. Gordon Peake is a research associate on the Warlords to Peacelords pro-

Gordon Peake, "Warlords to Peacelords," *Journal of International Affairs*, vol. 56, Spring 2003, pp. 182–89. Copyright © 2003 by The Trustees of Columbia University in the City of New York. Reproduced by permission.

ject at International Conflict Research at the University of Ulster in Northern Ireland.

It is almost a cliché to refer to many of the current [2003] crop of Afghani leaders as warlords. An evocative term, it conjures up a series of cinematic images of leadership in societies beset by protracted, violent conflict. With positions of power and authority organized around ethnic, tribal, sectional and clan lines, this type of leadership emerges from failed states where the structure, authority and power of the central government have either decayed or fragmented altogether. Beginning as a term to describe leaders in pre-Communist China, the label has also been assigned to leadership in Liberia, Somalia, Lebanon and Burma, among other places. Although the countries are geographically disparate, the traits exercised by such leaders are similar in a number of respects.

What Is a Warlord?

Warlords are characterized as leaders who control and police specific areas of territory within the state where the writ of the central government does not run. Their political ascendance is inextricably linked to their military power. Through either trade in extractive resources or the levying of taxes and duties, they exercise degrees of economic and political power, which often exceeds that of the country's central government. With a personal and charismatic form of leadership, a warlord's style is autocratic with little formal consultation.

Many in the current crop of Afghan leaders neatly fit this description. Rooting their legitimacy in their backgrounds as military commanders, many of Afghanistan's significant leaders have regional power and authority that collectively match—if not outweigh—that of the fledgling central administration, set up in December 2001 to replace the Taliban regime. Their role in the fall of the Taliban earned many of them high international profiles. Northern leader Abdul Rashid Dostum, Defense Minister Muhammad Fahim and Kandahar Governor Gul Agha Shirzai have name recognition matching that of the country's president, Hamid Karzai.

Amid the world's newfound attention on their leadership and the reconstruction of Afghanistan's government to a more representative and inclusive form, is it accurate to relabel these war-

lords as "peacelords"—a transition once envisioned, if not expected, by many? At this point, the assessment is bleak. In a country with a deep tradition of localized and personalized rule, the
prospect of a centralized government—the base around which
reconstruction efforts were to be harnessed in the aftermath of
the war against the Taliban—remains distant. Instead of becoming peacelords, many Afghan warlords are now closer to peace-
mongers. They retain control of their own areas in order to reap
the large economic gains and take benefits that suit them in the
process of their country's reconstruction, such as national title
and financial rewards, but they fail to contribute fully to the
achievement of lasting peace. Their relationship with the central
government is ambivalent at best.

So far, the various international actors in the country have
done little to halt this drift toward regionalization. Indeed, at
times their actions have even encouraged it. Having used some
leaders and their fighters as local proxies in the war against the
Taliban and Al Qaeda, the U.S. presidential administration continues to support these leaders on an individual basis, giving them
little incentive to centralize. Other international actors, most significantly the United Nations Assistance Mission in Afghanistan
(UNAMA), created to shepherd the country through the early
throes of reconstruction, have insufficient leverage to reverse this
tendency. Their mandate is too restrictive to have significant influence on political developments. They have neither carrot nor
stick to sway local leaders. It is a similar story with the large number of international development organizations that regularly liaise, consult and cooperate with local leaders.

Who Are the Leaders?

Most leaders' political prominence derives from their history
either as commanders of the *mujahedeen* in the war against the
Soviet-backed government or as leaders of militias. At the end
of the war, these leaders maintained existing positions of authority by retaining a loyal corps of fighters and distributing patronage through wages. By controlling security, a leader controls the
flow of trade and goods in and out of the area under his control.
With personal charisma, a leader builds up a client base, which
helps to accumulate the resources and funds required to cement
his position of authority. Through the intertwining of security
and business interests, local networks of dependence, influence

and allegiance developed, bound together by loyalties to family and tribe. In an area where the concept of the state as provider traditionally has been absent, allegiance and dependence have been given to local leaders rather than to the abstract nation state.

The localized nature of leadership and absence of state authority have thus been mutually reinforcing in Afghanistan. Over time, powerful regional interests that are developed prevent the creation of national institutions. Political calculations are made in light of local issues and their ramifications, while the principal incentives and causes for leaders to act are primarily rooted in their locality. Traditionally there have existed few reasons to bring national concern into one's reckonings: in Afghanistan, all politics is local.

The first experiences that many leaders had with governance did not bode well for their second tries. Many of today's ascendant leaders were abject failures during their previous incumbencies as components of the *mujahedeen* administrations that governed from 1992 to 1996. The conversion from overthrowing a government to administrating as part of one was not easy: it proved impossible to agree on a national government. Although they had been able to unite against a common foe, the resistance groups were unable to pursue a joint strategy for administration, and the country broke up into essentially autonomous spheres of local leadership. No one could resolve the squabbling over divvying up national posts among the leaders—a combination of personal rivalry heightened by ethnic and tribal difference—and they resorted to violence to settle their disputes. The capital fell under heavy shelling; the shattered cityscape continues to bear witness to the ferocity of the fighting. While estimates vary, some put the number of citizens who died during the period 1992 to 1996 as high as fifty thousand.

During the fighting, the capacity of the administration to govern was very limited. Beyond the capital, local power wielders continued in the tradition of autonomous control over the outlying cities, towns and regions. The norm continued to be local administrations, which were run with various degrees of competence, over national governance. In some areas of the country, however, particularly in the south, disorder flourished as former allies in the resistance fought local spats for ascendancy.

With large swathes of the country pitched into disorder, the Taliban movement, composed mainly of Afghan refugee students, emerged as an alternative. Receiving large-scale financial and logistical support from Pakistan, the movement took Kandahar in 1994, spreading throughout the southern portion of the country, eventually seizing control of Kabul in 1996. By year's end it had effective control over nine-tenths of the country. The Taliban restored security and order to the area, but it was a bleak and harsh regime. Enforcing an austere, anti-modernist interpretation of Islam, it banned women from employment and education. A catalogue of policies and prohibitions were imposed that ranged from public executions to a ban on kite flying.

In the wake of the Taliban's arrival, former leaders effectively faced two main choices: fight or flee. Those who stayed organized themselves under the banner of the Northern Alliance, an edgy coalition of forces consisting of leaders from the Tajik and Uzbek communities. While it succeeded in protecting a northern sliver of the country from Taliban control, the Alliance found it more difficult to recapture any territory. Barring the occasional territorial transfer, the map of Afghanistan changed little between 1996 and 2001. Some leaders left the country, relocating mainly to Pakistan, while others moved to the Persian Gulf and Europe. Formerly in the ascendancy, these leaders were essentially sidelined. It appeared that their chance to govern had passed.

September 11 and Its Consequences

The attacks of 11 September 2001 and the ensuing American-led war against the Taliban provided an unexpected opportunity for warlords to reassert their prominence. For many, it was yet another chance to serve in government. As the only coherent local force operating in Afghanistan, the Northern Alliance proved to be the natural partner for international operations against the Taliban. Flush with new supplies and cash and backed by a mammoth air bombardment, Northern Alliance troops swiftly captured city after city. Kabul fell in mid-November, and with it, symbolically, the Taliban regime itself.

The country and its leaders thus found themselves part of a new political landscape that they could not have shaped for themselves. Local leaders played little or no part in engineering the pace or nature of the transition from conflict to peace. While the Afghan leaders were the principal local beneficiaries of the change, the decision to make it had been taken by leaders of a country far more powerful than their own.

The question shifted to what form of administration should replace the Taliban. Merely allowing the Northern Alliance to install themselves as government leaders was not a viable option. Not only were they wholly unrepresentative of Afghanistan's largest ethnic group, the Pashtuns, but they also presented the risk that allowing them an untrammeled second try at government could be as fractious and disastrous as their first attempt. Under the auspices of the United Nations, it was decided to bring together representative groups in an attempt to forge an agreement on a new political architecture for the country. Meeting in Bonn,

PRESIDENT KARZAI'S INAUGURAL SPEECH

Hamid Karzai was elected president of Afghanistan in October 2004 in the country's first direct elections. The following is an excerpt from his inaugural speech.

During our election campaign, we presented a manifesto for the future to the people of Afghanistan. Our principal promises are concerning the strengthening of security sector and ensuring lasting stability throughout the country; the elimination of poppy cultivation and the fight against processing and trafficking of drugs; the disarmament and demobilisation of former combatants; the eradication of poverty, generation of wealth and the provision of public services especially to the rural areas; the rule of law, and the protection of civil liberties and human rights; the acceleration of administrative reform to strengthen administration, root out corruption, stop the abuse of public funds, and ensure meritocracy; the strengthening of national unity; the rebuilding and building of the country's infrastructure; and of course the strengthening of understanding and cooperation with the international community. We feel obliged to work to deliver on these promises, with the help of God the Almighty, over the next five years. . . .

Germany, four groups attended the talks. Along with the Northern Alliance, there were representatives of the Rome grouping and two smaller blocs known as the Cyprus and Peshawar groups. The Rome grouping, predominantly Pashtun, was identified with Afghanistan's former king Zahir Shah while the other two were backed by Iran and Pakistan, respectively.

Ignoring the historical tradition of a feeble center and strong periphery, the agreement aspired to reestablish and empower the country's long-dormant state institutions. The "agreement on provisional arrangements in Afghanistan pending the reestablish-

---

I must hasten to say that our fight against terrorism is not yet over, even though we have succeeded to reduce this common enemy of humanity to a lesser threat in this country. The relationship between terrorism and narcotics, and the continued threat of extremism in the region and the world at large, are a source of continued concern. A decisive victory over terrorism requires serious and continued cooperation at regional and international levels.

Three years ago [in 2001], the firm and productive cooperation of the international cooperation rid Afghanistan from the rule of terrorism. The same cooperation has led to the rebuilding of the Afghan state, and significant progress in restoring peace, stability and security to our country. As a result, we have now left a hard and dark past behind us, and today we are opening a new chapter in our history, in a spirit of friendship with the international community. . . .

Last week, during a meeting with the elders of Badghis province, as I went around greeting the guests individually, I saw an elderly man who had tears in his eyes and said to me as I shook his hand: "We want a clean and efficient government from you!" I would like all of you to leave this gathering today having heard one pledge from me: I will do everything it takes to turn that elderly man's tears of hope into the smile of fulfillment.

Hamid Karzai, presidential inaugural speech, December 7, 2004.

ment of permanent government institutions," to be known as the Bonn Agreement, mapped out a two-step plan to achieve that goal over two years.

In the first step, an interim Afghan authority was established. Its immediate tenure would run for six months, to be followed by the convening of a *loya jirga*—a special council of mandated Afghan notables—which would decide further on the makeup of the transitional government. Elections would be held at the end of the period.

Results of the Bonn Agreement

The Bonn Agreement included many of the most powerful regional commanders in the government. Cabinet posts were given to some, and senior regional positions to others. Although a Pashtun, Hamid Karzai headed the government, members of the Northern Alliance were given the most powerful jobs. The military head of the Alliance, Marshal Muhammad Fahim, was granted the defense portfolio. Other senior figures, such as Abdallah Abdallah and Younis Qanooni, were given foreign and interior affairs portfolios respectively. Powerful northern leader Abdul Rashid Dostum, whose forces had been instrumental in the overthrow, was appointed Deputy Defense Minister. In the absence of viable alternatives, a deal was made with regional leaders, who were slated to be the base to begin the hewing of a civilian form of politics. For a country shattered by decades of war it was a momentous task for the nascent administration, largely because a major part of the deal's success was dependent on leaders undergoing the profound transition from warlord to peacelord.

The agreement also provided for international assistance. The International Security Assistance Force (ISAF) would help provide security in and around the capital, while UNAMA would be mobilized to assist the transitional administration in reconstruction. Unlike previous missions, such as the United Nations Interim Administration Mission in Kosovo (UNMIK) and the United Nations Transitional Administration in East Timor (UNTAET), where the UN was the effective administrator and de facto ruler, the mission to Afghanistan would have a more limited mandate. Aiming to leave an institutional "light footprint," the UN would assist but would not dictate the direction and shape of change [according to scholar Simon Chesterman].

The *loya jirga* confirmed the ascendancy of regional leaders in the cabinet and the political dominance of the Northern Alliance. There were few significant changes in cabinet shape, even amid indications that regional leaders had influenced the election of council delegates. According to Human Rights Watch, the regional leaders threatened violence if they did not receive the ministerial titles they desired. Despite impassioned entreaties from delegates about the undue influence of regional leaders, their political influence was bolstered.

Central Government Is Still an Illusion

Beyond public professions of loyalty, many of the leaders have assumed ministerial titles without deviating from an agenda to work toward cementing positions of local ascendancy. As a result, over a year after its inauguration, the concept of a central government remains largely phantasmal outside of the capital. Power continues to be localized, resting with a range of local actors. The majority is comprised of those leaders who "backed the right horse" in the months after the September 11 attacks, namely those militia commanders who allied with the American forces during the war against the Taliban. With their militias controlling local security, these leaders run civil administrations, levy duties and keep taxes. Political and economic power, afforded to them by effective autonomy over large tracts of land, serves as a disincentive to join the central administration: if they did, the consequent loss of independent revenue streams would weaken their local position.

Securing local dominance is foremost in warlords' calculations, and their willingness to use violence to achieve their goals has resulted in clashes throughout the country. These quarrels, continuing without reference to the central government, are a potent sign of the government's quintessential weakness. Although President Karzai has, in public statements and government edicts, grown increasingly vociferous in his calls for regional leaders to desist, rein themselves in and sign up to be part of the government, his admonitions ring hollow. These statements cannot be backed up due to the lack of a strong national army. Although one is in the early stages of creation, it will take at least three more years to take shape. Even then, the question looms large as to where the ultimate loyalty of many of its recruits will lie, as they are likely to be drawn from the ranks of fighters from warlord militias. The writ of the national police does not extend beyond Kabul. Neither does that of the ISAF. The weak government is thus incapable of appeasing or threatening regional leaders to induce their support; regional leaders are the key to strengthening the government, but they have little incentive to do so.

The political makeup of the northern province of Balkh—one of the areas outside of the effective control of the central government—illustrates the strong regional nature of politics and consequent difficulty of creating the web of governance to which Bonn aspired. Centered around the city of Mazar-i-Sharif, clashes continue in Balkh between the two nominal partners in the central government, Abdul Rashid Dostum and Atta Muhammad.

When he was appointed deputy defense minister, Dostum was assigned to oversee the construction of a national army. One year later, that idea is still in its infancy, and he has not dismantled his large private army, which is still used as the principal instrument in his battle with Atta Muhammad's Jamiat-i-Islami faction for political control over the northern region. Despite the brokering of several ceasefires, clashes have continued. In a sign of the distribution of power in the region, the governor appointed by the central government is regarded as third in the rankings of political importance.

All of the leaders in the north have backgrounds in armed deeds. Atta and the governor, Haji Muhammad Ishaq Rah Gosar, were both senior *mujahedeen* commanders. Dostum commanded a militia allied with the Afghan national army. All three retained private armies after the departure of the Soviets and used them to build their legitimacy and power. The governor explained:

> It was my long history as a leader in the holy war (*jihad*) against the Soviets that gave me the regard of my people. The people have seen that and respect me for it. For sure fighting was not a good thing. During the period people were deprived of their schooling and we have large numbers of martyrs, widows, amputees and cripples. Leading through these adversity and deprivations, however, has also taught us skills.

Atta concurred, "I have no regrets about my past. It was the best way of education about how to be organized and so it teaches one how to govern."

The northern area is run as an entity almost totally separate from the central government. Basic services such as schools and health centers are funded by a combination of resources from regional leaders and international aid. Regional power holders even receive kudos and publicity by subsidizing the running of certain governmental offices. Patronage distributed through the provision of services makes the leaders' support networks stronger. The Ministry of Women's Affairs in Balkh Province, for instance, is furnished and funded by Atta Muhammad. In interviews [with the author], some of the representatives were fulsome in praise of the local leader.

The International Community Will Play a Major Role

In order to rein local leaders in, continual application of pressure from the international community is necessary. Currently, the manner in which international leverage is being used serves only to maintain regionalization. Much of the power and authority that many regional leaders currently enjoy is a side effect of U.S. antiterrorism efforts in Afghanistan. American troops and intelligence agents initially distributed cash and weapons to the leaders in order to enlist their help in overthrowing the Taliban, and still use them in the search for leadership and foot soldiers of Al Qaeda and their local supporters. Strengthened by new supplies, the leaders benefit much more from their own areas than from joining the central government. Patronage, in return for utilization of local knowledge, continues to sway local leaders away from signing up to be part of the central governmental structures.

The dispersion of power into regional tracts has profound implications for the country's recovery from conflict. It is a direct obstacle to coordinated reconstruction efforts. International aid agencies are torn between dealing with powerless employees of the Afghan government and regional leaders, upon whose acquiescence they depend to get anything done. The power of local leaders, coupled with the absence of any meaningful alternative, means that international agencies are forced to liaise with them, thus strengthening their hold. The UN, charged with aiding Afghan reconstruction, does not have the authority to boss local political leaders around. One senior official lamented:

> What we have just done is we have gone against the tide of history. . . . [T]his is not a historically unique phe-

nomenon. You will find that there are plenty of civil wars when you go through the stages; main struggle, achieve the goal, get into a system of anarchy, a vacuum emerges and then somebody arises to fill the vacuum. Nobody gives these guys a second chance, no one ever gets a second chance; it is once only. It's an even more difficult task to rebuild now, and they made a hash of it the first time around. The Americans had a clearly limited agenda, a military agenda, which was to topple the Taliban, but they have not put enough thought into the more difficult task of what would come after.

The Taliban Is Attempting to Regain Control of Afghanistan

By Phil Zabriskie

On September 11, 2001, the world was shocked when the Twin Towers in midtown Manhattan were brought to the ground by terrorists who flew commercial airplanes into them. The terrorists were members of al Qaeda, an Islamic group sheltered by Afghanistan's tyrannical Islamic government, the Taliban. The terrorist attack was a turning point for the U.S. government, which quickly launched an all-out effort to catch the terrorist leaders and destroy their ability to operate. These efforts included a war on Afghanistan to topple the Taliban government, which refused to surrender al Qaeda leader Osama bin Laden, whom it was protecting. The United States began providing arms and monetary support to the Northern Alliance, a diverse group of mujahideen armies that were fighting the Taliban on the ground. The United States also began bombing Taliban strongholds. By late 2001 the Taliban had been driven from power. The United States and the UN helped install an interim government and began to try to reestablish order in the country. The restrictions that the Taliban had imposed began to be lifted: Women could be seen in public without their all-enveloping burkas, people could play music and hang pictures, and men could shave their beards.

However, the Taliban had not been eradicated. By mid-2003 surviving members were regrouping in Pakistan and were launching attacks on U.S. military bases and Afghan cities. In the following selection, Time *magazine reporter Phil Zabriskie describes the Taliban's attempts to regain power in Afghanistan and the efforts of Afghanistan's new government to repel them.*

Phil Zabriskie, "Undefeated," *Time Asia,* vol. 162, July 21, 2003. Copyright © 2003 by Time, Inc. All rights reserved. Reproduced by permission.

Commander Mamabaidullah switches off the ignition and alights from his pickup truck onto the desert plain surrounding Spin Boldak, a chaotic Afghan town that borders Pakistan. Followed by four of his Kalashnikov [rifle] toting men, he walks briskly toward a graveyard where scores of bodies lie buried beneath mounds of dirt and clay. Mamabaidullah, who is responsible for guarding this stretch of frontier between Afghanistan and Pakistan, stops at the row closest to the border. With evident pride, he explains that they contain the corpses of Taliban militiamen killed by Afghan soldiers during a battle last month [June 2003]. These Taliban, Mamabaidullah says, had been hiding in Pakistan and returned to attack a government office in a nearby village. Officially, 40 Taliban died in the ensuing firefight, though a source present at the encounter and an official in Kabul both put the death toll, which included seven Afghan soldiers, nearer to 90. It was one of the Taliban's biggest defeats since they were toppled in December 2001. Mamabaidullah had these bodies buried here to send a message "that if anyone comes into Afghanistan to kill or make problems, they'll end up like this."

The Taliban, however, show no intention of heeding his crude warning. In the past month [July 2003], militants belonging to or affiliated with the Taliban have launched scores of rockets at U.S. military bases and detonated explosives in several Afghan cities. They have ambushed American and Afghan troops and torched newly rebuilt schools. During the last week of June, Taliban combatants temporarily seized government offices in a remote part of Zabul province. On June 30 a Taliban operative planted an antipersonnel mine in a Kandahar mosque run by a pro-government cleric; the subsequent blast wounded 17 worshipers. The next day, an anti-Taliban mullah was killed by a shot to the head.

A year ago, notes Masood Khalili, once a leader of the anti-Taliban Northern Alliance and now Afghanistan's ambassador to India, "the Taliban were scared, broken and disconcerted. Now they are forming again, slowly, gradually, like a photograph developing." The big picture, according to Kandahar's police chief Brigadier General Mohammed Akram, is that "the Taliban are stronger now than at any time since the fall of their government." These neo-Taliban number in the "thousands," according to an Afghan security official in Kabul. They operate primarily out of Pakistan, guided by many of the same men—including supreme leader Mullah Mohammed Omar—who ran Afghanistan's ultra-orthodox theocracy from 1995 through 2001, when the group harbored [terrorist leader] Osama bin Laden and lent eager support to al-Qaeda. While maintaining close ties to al-Qaeda, the Taliban have also forged a deepening alliance with Afghan warlord Gulbuddin Hekmatyar and his fundamentalist, vehemently anti–Western Hizb-i-Islami party, which remains potent in eastern Afghanistan. Afghan government officials, including President Hamid Karzai, and members of the U.S.-led Joint Coalition Task Force have downplayed recent attacks. Karzai tells *Time* that the Taliban are not regrouping: "Any internal danger is from terrorism and from al-Qaeda organizing from outside." Coalition spokesman Colonel Rodney Davis agrees: "The coalition has degraded what was a formidable force." True enough. But the Taliban have taken what was left of their own army and morphed it into a guerrilla-and-terror outfit. Their goal, says Afghanistan expert Professor Barnett Rubin of New York University's (NYU) Center on International Cooperation, is to "cause enough terror that the foreigners will leave Afghanistan and Afghans will be afraid to collaborate with the government in Kabul, causing it to crumble." That's likely beyond their reach, but in a country as unstable as Afghanistan, even degraded Taliban fighters are a lethal threat.

Mamabaidullah's office overlooks one of this battle's front lines: Spin Boldak's main border checkpoint, a notorious smugglers' route from the Pakistani town of Chaman. Entering or leaving the country often requires no papers at all. "It's impossible to control," says Khalid Pashtoon, spokesman for Kandahar Governor Gul Agha Sherzai. It's also the Taliban's gateway to revenge. Following their ouster from Afghanistan, most Taliban leaders found sanctuary among fellow ethnic Pashtuns in Pakistan's lawless Baluchistan and North-West Frontier Province (N.W.F.P.) regions. Pakistani authorities have arrested nearly 500 suspected al-Qaeda members, but Karzai, among others, has charged that the U.S.'s avowed ally has shown little inclination to apprehend top-level Taliban, even when provided addresses where they could be found. "If we had sincere and honest cooperation from Pakistan," charges the security official in Kabul, "there'd be no Taliban threat in Afghanistan." After the battle near Spin Boldek, Mamabaidullah made the point less delicately by piling more than 20 bodies onto a dump truck, driving to the border and depositing them on Pakistani soil.

Faisal Saleh Hayat, Pakistan's Interior Minister, insists that "our focus is equally on al-Qaeda and on the Taliban." President Pervez Musharraf has praised his security forces for capturing 10 Taliban leaders. He also sent Pakistani soldiers into parts of N.W.F.P. where they hadn't been "for over a century." But that late-June campaign stemmed from reports that bin Laden was in the area. A Pakistani intelligence source near Chaman says his orders are "not to harass nor appease" the Taliban but to let them be.

Essentially, the Taliban have returned to the cradle in which they were nurtured a decade ago with funding and training by Pakistan's powerful Inter-Services Intelligence agency (ISI). (Accusations persist that rogue ISI agents or ex-agents still back the Taliban.) The border provinces are controlled by Jamiat Ulema Islam, an extremist party that openly harbors the Taliban. In Quetta, 110 kilometers southeast of Chaman, men roam the streets wearing the distinctive black or white robes and black or white turbans characteristic of the Taliban. "We feel relaxed and safe here," says a young Talib. A local cleric says Taliban commanders meet regularly in the town to plan raids into their former domain. Foot soldiers "operate in twos and threes," says a trader who works on both sides of the border. "They sneak across, carry out attacks and come back."

Mullah Omar himself is believed to be moving throughout Baluchistan and southwestern Afghanistan. Taliban spokesman Mohammed Mukhtar Mujahid, who is also at large, says Omar communicates with acolytes via recorded or written messages. Mujahid recently announced that Omar had formed a ten-man "leadership council" and assigned each lieutenant a specific region to destabilize. This guerrilla war cabinet includes Saifur Rahman Mansoor, who led Taliban forces against British and U.S. troops during Operation Anaconda in early 2002, and Mullah Dadullah Akhund, the one-legged intelligence chief who ordered the execution of a Salvadorean International Committee of the Red Cross worker in Uruzgan province in March [2003]. While rallying old soldiers, the Taliban are also recruiting new members, targeting disgruntled young Afghans in refugee camps in Chaman, Quetta, Peshawar and Karachi. The appeals play on pride and alienation, charging that the Americans are denigrating Islam and Pashtuns. "You are seeing the picture of a dirty Jewish infidel searching the body of a Muslim woman," reads a flyer found in Chaman, which shows a Western soldier frisking a burqa-clad female. "If a Muslim does not display his feelings by defending his faith and honor, then he is not a Muslim nor an Afghan."

Karzai favors reintegrating low-level Taliban into Afghan society. But Mullah Khaksar, an ex-Taliban minister who later allied himself with the Northern Alliance, says Talibs are warned by their peers that "they'll be sent to Guantánamo" [a U.S. military prison located on the island of Cuba] if they return. Or, he adds, "[the Taliban] pay people to join their jihad." Mullah Nik Mohammed, a Taliban commander captured in Spin Boldak, told his interrogators that he would have received $850 for detonating a bomb, double that if it killed a civilian, and $2,600 for taking a soldier's life.

The Taliban's most dangerous ally, however, appears to be the warlord Hekmatyar. He, like the Taliban leaders, is a Pashtun with a fundamentalist interpretation of Islam and a hatred for the Americans and Karzai. His guerrilla fighting skills seduced the CIA and Pakistan into giving him billions of dollars of support and arms during the Soviet occupation. In May 2002, however, the U.S. tried to kill him with a Hellfire missile strike, and coalition soldiers have launched several operations in his traditional strongholds of Nangarhar and Kunar provinces. A diplomat in Kabul believes Taliban leaders don't trust Hekmatyar, whose treachery is legendary even by the spectacularly duplicitous standards of Afghan warfare. But a former Taliban financier in Chaman says Hizb-i-Islami has forged lies with "mid-ranking commanders and ordinary Taliban," providing cash and motorcycles for cross-border attacks.

Singapore-based al-Qaeda expert Rohan Gunaratna asserts that the two groups are much more closely linked, that bin Laden himself oversaw the formation of their alliance "soon after U.S. troops entered Afghanistan. But now this understanding has become very deep. There's integration between the organizations." It amounts to a division of labor: the Taliban focus on southern Afghanistan and Hizb-i-Islami on the east, which frees al-Qaeda "to use its limited strength for operations overseas," explains Gunaratna. (Several U.S. and Afghan intelligence sources, however, suspect al-Qaeda engineered a June 7 [2003] suicide bombing in Kabul that killed four German peacekeeping soldiers and an Afghan teenager.)

Outgunned on the home front, the Taliban mainly engage in hit-and-run skirmishes. Sergeant David Smith, who is stationed at a U.S. firebase in Paktika province, says his unit has encountered amateur warriors who forgot to pull the pins from the grenades they threw. But the unit has also faced highly trained professional soldiers. Recalling a clash in April [2003], he says, "Those guys knew what they were doing. I have to give 'em props."

Facing a more elusive enemy, coalition forces are also trying to adapt—by increasing their humanitarian efforts. Four Provincial Reconstruction Teams have been deployed by U.S. and British forces. They patrol, liaise with local leaders and work with NGOs [nongovernmental organizations] to distribute school and building supplies, dig wells and repair bridges. "It is crucial," says Colonel Davis, "that we show measurable, visible progress in terms of stability and reconstruction." A school or clinic built by the coalition, NGOs or local government can have a huge impact on a village, providing not only services but also a rebuttal to the Taliban's call to jihad. In Tani, a village in Khost province a few kilometers from the border with Pakistan, parents say school enrollment has doubled, and a 14-year-old boy excitedly describes a curriculum that now includes science, math and English. At a fruit stand in Logar province, Shakur, 60, says his village now has a medical clinic. The Taliban, he says, "did nothing for this country."

But the hope generated by billions of dollars in promised aid has been dampened by the lack of significant progress on large-scale, job-producing projects such as repairing the nation's horrendous roads. Meanwhile, the country continues to suffer from numerous potentially crippling problems: corruption and lawlessness are pervasive; civil servants often don't get paid; Karzai's power is largely limited to Kabul; warlords rule the countryside; the Afghan National Army is years from being a legitimate security force; and Finance Minister Ashraf Ghani is warning that the massive proliferation of poppy production [the poppy flower is used to produce heroin] threatens to turn Afghanistan into a narco-state. Among many diplomats, aid workers and Afghan officials, there is a growing sense of foreboding. "Everyone can see very little is happening and that, evidently, the U.S. is not serious about its so-called commitment to reconstruct Afghanistan," says NYU's Professor Rubin. A recent Council on Foreign Relations and Asia Society report, *Afghanistan: Are We Losing the Peace?*, warns, "Failure to stem deteriorating security conditions and to spur economic reconstruction could lead to a reversion to warlord-dominated anarchy and mark a major defeat for the U.S. war on terrorism."

Gunaratna, for one, believes a revitalized Taliban operating with relative freedom in Pakistan not only undermines the new Afghan government but also feeds the risk of terrorism abroad. "Al-Qaeda is able to survive because of its link with the Taliban," he says. In short, they are still harboring al-Qaeda—but in Pakistan, not Afghanistan.

For the Taliban, there is currency in every gripe, every unfulfilled promise, every report of American troops kicking in doors during village raids, every hired gun looking for work. "Just returning to Afghanistan is a victory for the Taliban," says Masood Khalili, Kabul's ambassador to India. But they clearly want more. "We are waiting," says Qari Rehman, a Talib in Chaman. "You will see. The situation will get worse."

Many Afghan Citizens Live in Fear of a New Drug War

By Christian Parenti

In 2000 the Taliban regime in Afghanistan banned the cultivation of opium poppies, stopping 90 percent of the farming of the lucrative crop. However, since the United States went to war against the Taliban in 2001 and drove the fundamentalist Islamic leaders from power, the cultivation of poppies has of poppies has returned with a vengeance. In the following selection, journalist Christian Parenti describes the growth of poppy farming in Afghanistan. He points out that Afghanistan has been left in ruins by decades of war and recent droughts and that its people are desperate to survive, by illegal means if necessary. Afghan farmers can earn far more from growing poppies than from wheat or other traditional crops, and many mujahideen commanders are also involved in the opium drug trade. Until recently, the United States has ignored the growing drug trade in Afghanistan, Parenti notes. But in 2004 American officials announced U.S. intentions to begin to eradicate poppy cultivation. Many poor Afghans fear that their livelihoods will be destroyed if their crops are eliminated. Parenti also points out that a war on the opium drug trade could cause the mujahideen warlords who have supported the U.S. occupation of the country to turn against the United States. Christian Parenti is the author of The Freedom: Shadows and Hallucinations in Occupied Iraq.

The rotund landlord, Mr. Attock, sits on the carpeted floor of his little office and living quarters in Jalalabad, Afghanistan. From this one room he publishes a slight and sporadic weekly or sometimes monthly newspaper, but like most

Christian Parenti, "Afghan Poppies Bloom," *The Nation*, vol. 280, January 24, 2005, p. 22. Copyright © 2005 by The Nation Company LP. Reproduced by permission.

people around here, his real business is farming opium poppy. Mr. Attock's land lies about an hour and a half away in the country-side of Nangarhar province, near the Pakistani border, not too far from Tora Bora.

"My dear, everyone grows poppy. Even me," says Mr. Attock in slightly awkward English as he leans over to grab my leg, again. Mr. Attock is a bundle of physical and intellectual energy, not all of it well focused. "My dear, you see. Listen. My dear, wheat is worthless. Everyone grows poppy. We will go to my village and you will see."

The next day we tour the village where Mr. Attock owns or manages a farm (it's not entirely clear who actually owns the es-tablishment, but he is in charge). Nangarhar is one of Afghanistan's top three drug-producing provinces. The surrounding fields rotate between corn and poppies. Mr. Attock says he has almost 100 people living and working here as tenant farmers and laborers.

For the past three years [since 2001], growing poppy in Af-ghanistan, as Mr. Attock and his tenants do, has been a relatively risk-free and open business. The Taliban had imposed a ruthlessly successful ban on poppy cultivation in 2000; more than 90 per-cent of cultivation stopped. But since the US invasion in 2001, eradication efforts have been minimal and ineffective and pro-duction has again soared.

A Billion-Dollar Trade

Globally, Afghanistan's opium business is estimated to be worth more than $30 billion a year, with the vast majority of that cash being captured by players in other countries. One Western coun-ternarcotics official estimated that poppy production increased by 64 percent in 2004. Afghanistan now produces an estimated 87 percent of the world's opium, most of which becomes heroin and morphine. Income from poppy and its associated processing and trafficking are said to contribute $2.8 billion annually to the Afghan economy, a sum equal to 60 percent of the country's le-gitimate GDP [gross domestic product]. About a quarter of this money ends up in the hands of common farmers; the rest goes to traffickers. UN researchers believe that 2.3 million of Afghanistan's 20–25 million people are directly involved in poppy cultivation, with many more working in processing, trafficking, moneylend-ing, laundering and other associated activities. The warlords who run this country tax both farmers and traffickers alike.

The British, who are part of the international coalition now occupying Afghanistan, have been in charge of establishing a Counter
Narcotics Directorate in Kabul. Its efforts have not been aggressive,
and until recently the Americans have openly avoided the issue of
poppy cultivation, preferring to focus instead on hunting down the
Taliban and Al Qaeda and training the new Afghan National
Army. But after three years of ignoring poppy cultivation and
heroin production, the United States has suddenly changed course.
In mid-November [2004], Washington pledged $780 million to-
ward Afghanistan's war on drugs. If a rigorous campaign against
poppy actually materializes, it could radically destabilize the relative calm that now obtains in much of Afghanistan.

Already there is trouble brewing in Nangarhar, where next
year's crop is just starting to sprout. Farmers report low-flying
planes spraying poison on their fields. Doctors in the area say
they've seen a sudden jump in respiratory illness and skin rashes,
while veterinarians are seeing sickened livestock. In a harbinger
of what a real war on drugs might bring, one farmer in Nangarhar whose son had been poisoned by the spraying told a local
journalist, "If my son dies, I will join the Taliban, and I will kill
as many Americans as I can find."

Growing Opium

Nangarhar's provincial governor, a former mujahedeen commander named Haji Din Mohammed, has said there is "no doubt that
an aerial spray has taken place." Other Afghan officials have called
it illegal. The United States controls Afghan airspace but denies
that it has sprayed, though it is promising a "robust" eradication
campaign come spring.

Mr. Attock is reveling in his role as country squire and host. At
his village we sit on cots made of rope and wood to eat a break-
fast of thick clotted butter cream, honey and flat bread, washed
down with lots of sweet tea. As I wait beneath a huge tree in the
courtyard of Mr. Attock's kala, a fortress-like family compound,
he corrals three farmers and tells them to fetch opium and opium
seeds, to take seats and to explain the trade to his guest.

The three farmers, all of them lean and sinewy and looking a
bit skeptical, take seats and politely start talking shop. For the most
part, growing opium in Afghanistan is like growing any other
crop. Though technically illicit, it's all rather undramatic: Farmers are concerned with irrigation, weather, pests, disease and

prices. Their tasks are similarly prosaic, consisting mainly of weeding, watering and tending the crops.

The most talkative and inquisitive farmer is Abdul Rakmon. For every few questions from me he has one of his own. "Have you been to Fremont, California? Some people from around here live there now. Where exactly is Fremont?"

Rakmon and his less talkative mates explain that in the warm climate of Nangarhar there is one crop of poppy, though in other areas there are two seasons, the second less productive than the first. In Nangarhar the land is fertilized with manure in late October, and then the poppy seeds are sown in November. By February the flowers bloom, then the blossoms fall away to reveal a bulging seedpod. In March the farmers start harvesting the opium by cutting or scraping the seedpods with small trowels.

From the little scrape wounds oozes a sticky white sap—raw opium. The milk-colored opium turns brown with exposure to air. In Nangarhar the farmers cut the seedpods in the evening and collect the congealed sap in the morning.

"We cut the seedpod with a ghoza," says Rakmon, and he gives me a little wooden tool with a serrated metal edge. "You can have this ghoza as a present. People in New York will be impressed when they see that," he says with a grin. He's making a sage but cryptic comment on the huge physical, but even greater social, distance between heroin's site of production and its site of consumption. In front of us sits a big sickly-sweet-smelling block of opium.

Mr. Attock has become bored with the interviews and is done eating. He struts around the dusty courtyard, occasionally hoisting himself up off the ground on a tree branch. He wants my colleague, the photographer Teru Kuwayama, to take snapshots of his buildings and retinue of friends and employees from the village.

"What is his name? He looks like a Hazara," says Attock, referring to the Afghan ethnic minority known for their East Asian facial features.

"His name is Teru."

"Yes, OK. Steve!" shouts Mr. Attock, still unable to get Teru's name right. "Steve! Come. Take photos." The farmers tell me that the flowers come in red, white and purple. "Red flowers are the best," says Rakmon. In cooler climates other farmers inform me that white blossoms are superior.

Rakmon and his two friends explain that in most parts of Afghanistan a farmer can get up to seven collections from each seedpod.

Eventually the plant is tapped out and left to dry. The desiccated seedpods are harvested for next year's planting and the seeds are used to make edible oil. Mothers sometimes boil the dry pods into a tea that they use to drug their infants during long hours of work, or when the children are sick or hungry and unable to sleep.

"We Have No Choice but to Grow Poppy"

To illustrate the financial plight that drives people here to grow poppy—which, as good Muslims, they see as a sin—the farmers explain the math of poppy versus wheat. The local unit of land measurement here, a jerib, is roughly half an acre; and this part of Afghanistan is so close to Pakistan that commerce is conducted in Pakistani rupees instead of afghanis.

"It costs 1,000 rupees to plant one jerib of poppy, and that one jerib will yield at least fifteen kilograms of poppy, which is worth 300,000 Pakistani rupees [$5,000], at least," says a farmer named Lal Mohammed. (Later in the central highlands, some farmers tell me they can get twenty-eight kilos of opium per jerib.) "Wheat takes twice as long as poppy to grow, and we can buy almost ten times as much wheat as we could produce if we grow poppy instead," says Mohammed. "We have no choice but to grow poppy."

To top it all off, Afghanistan is in the midst of a hellacious six-year drought. Unlike wheat and vegetables or cotton, poppy is very drought-resistant. "All it really needs is a little water early on," says Mohammed.

The farmers confirm what I've heard elsewhere: The opium boom of the past three years has delivered many farmers from onerous debts and allowed them to keep land that they would otherwise have been forced to sell off to the local mujahedeen commanders.

After all the details of poppy growing are explained, Mr. Attock takes us on a tour of his village and invites me to shoot at a tree with one of his double-barreled shotguns. "Into the leaves, my dear. Up into the leaves. Yes!" The tree survives. Then we have more tea.

Later about six of us pack into a little Toyota four-wheel drive and slowly bounce and lurch down a sandy road lined with tall reeds through a string of small villages. At one of these clusters of mud-walled compounds we stop, interview another group of farmers about local politics and opium, then have a lunch of greasy rice and lamb and smoke hash with our hosts. This is haram, forbidden, in Islam. But way out here, is Allah really counting the minor indiscretions? Apparently some farmers think not.

On the dirt road back to Jalalabad, we stop to take photos. Around the bend rolls a small convoy of menacing US Special Forces, all mirrored sunglasses, beards and guns. The dreamy afternoon starts to feel creepy and not safe.

In the central highlands of Wardak province—which along with Nangarhar is one of the top opium-producing areas in Afghanistan and set to be targeted in the upcoming American-led eradication efforts—a different group of poppy farmers explains other aspects of the trade and the process of smuggling.

Teru and I are visiting friends of his who live in a series of picturesque villages strung out along a stunningly beautiful valley—lush and green at the bottom but hemmed in by huge, dry rocky mountains.

The family we're staying with is fairly prosperous, with some brothers and cousins working in Kabul, others involved in trucking and many others farming the valley's abundantly watered land. We spend most of our time drinking tea, cracking jokes and eating. There's growing political tension around here, so our hosts allow us to take only one hike. Nor do they want too many people to see them wandering around with foreigners.

Smugglers Take the Biggest Risks

I ask the farmers here about loans, because debt is said to be one of the ways big traffickers control little farmers. "No, no. The smugglers do not lend money," says a man named Nazir. "Mostly we have to borrow from merchants in the bazaar. You have to come up with your own money." Western experts had told me the smugglers make cash loans that are repaid at 100 percent interest, but in opium instead of cash. The system in Wardak seems to be less onerous, more streamlined, less formalized. And it externalizes risk for the lenders: Farmers purchase on credit from shopkeepers to survive, then repay in cash after payment from smugglers.

"Why would the smugglers want to lend us money? They know we have to grow poppy to survive," says Nazir, sounding like he wishes he could get a cash loan instead of store credit.

"The smugglers who take the opium away have the most dangerous job, you know. They get robbed. The commanders and police can attack them. It's very dangerous," says Nazir. "The worst that happens to farmers is their crops get destroyed. And this year we lost most of our poppy to disease anyway."

Nazir and his cousins say that the smaller smugglers tend to sell their loads to wholesalers, who often work with the authorities and use official vehicles and state-issued travel documents to move their consolidated loads into Iran and Pakistan. But such cover isn't always necessary.

"The border at Chaman, in Pakistan, is wide open," says one of Nazir's cousins. "I've crossed there without talking to anyone. You just drive across."

To turn opium into heroin it must be boiled down with lye to make morphine, then further refined with other chemicals. Western counternarcotics specialists and UN researchers say that Afghan opium has typically been processed into heroin by labs in Pakistan. But with the new opium boom, these labs are said to be moving into Afghanistan, making the smuggling operations more efficient and profitable. The guys in Wardak say there are some small labs in the area around their group of villages.

"Some young people smoke heroin, about 100 of them around here. That's a big problem for us," says a man named Hazrad. He speaks English, which most of his cousins can't understand too well. "They dip cigarettes in it and just smoke it. Some of them steal to get money." When I ask how the community is dealing with this he grows reticent and uncomfortable.

According to the farmers, the route into Pakistan seems to rely heavily on concealment within other commodities like wheat and rice or in fuel tankers, and the official border crossing is used. Smuggling into Iran is usually done with long, well-armed convoys of trucks or camels that try to avoid, or if necessary outgun, any Iranian border police they might meet. Violent clashes are routine, and Tehran reports that it has lost 3,100 security personnel over the past two decades in battles with well-armed and organized smugglers on the Afghan border. Almost 200 soldiers and 800 traffickers were killed in 2003 alone.

The United States Steps Up Its War on Drugs

When I ask about US plans to target Wardak in the spring of 2005, Nazir and the others grow concerned. "We have many former Taliban and mujahedeen commanders here who are getting angry at America because of what is happening in Palestine and Iraq and because the economy here is no good," says Nazir. "Cutting down poppy will only make them more angry." Already violence is on the rise in Wardak. People who work with the occupying forces are starting to be targeted by unknown assassins.

If poppy eradication threatens instability in Afghanistan, why is the United States now stepping up its war on drugs? Officially, the counternarcotics wonks in Kabul give all the right ethical arguments: Poppy is an evil fueling everything from Islamic terrorism to the spread of HIV.

But the poppy revival has also been clearly linked to a decline in rural indebtedness and an improvement in the status and standard of living of many women. Because opium harvesting is both labor-intensive and lucrative, it provides economic opportunities for Afghan women, many of whom either cultivate poppy on their own land or work as relatively well compensated wage laborers in the fields of others. The average wage for gathering opium can be as high as $7 a day. In Kabul a day laborer who works on a construction site or hauls goods can expect to make only $3 a day.

And the practice of turning a blind eye to the opium industry has functioned as a de facto development strategy in Afghanistan: It is probable that ordinary Afghans receive more income from drugs than they do from all the international aid they receive.

But across the planet in Washington, Afghanistan's poppy crop is viewed through the lens of reactionary moralism and domestic political theater rather than imperial pragmatism. And now powerful politicians want a better Afghan drug war.

The first demands came in 2003, when Republican Representative Henry Hyde sent a high-profile letter to Defense Secretary Donald Rumsfeld expressing his "growing concern about Afghanistan and the impact of illicit drugs on the fight against global terrorism."

This plea seemed to bear fruit. On a surprise visit to Kabul in August 2004, Rumsfeld singled out drugs as a problem "too serious to be ignored." In turn, the US ambassador to Afghanistan, Zalmay Khalilzad, said he expected "some broadening" of the US-led coalition's military efforts against poppy.

A Western official in Kabul told me that the United States was indeed ramping up its war on drugs and building a "pretty full partnership with the UK and Afghan government." He said that economic aid of between $30 million and $40 million had already arrived and would soon be invested in antipoppy economic development, or "the alternative livelihoods program." This scheme will involve creating cold storage facilities, communications links and improved roads, all with the aim of connecting traditional crops such as apples and raisins to world markets. But even the program's proponents admit that "nothing will replace opium." This bit of carrot will then be followed by the stick: an aggressive campaign of crop eradication to begin in February [2005].

"In 2005 eradication will be considerably more robust. At least five times as much poppy will be cut down as compared to last year," said the official, who spoke on the condition that he not be identified.

The Mujahedeen Could Withdraw Its Support of the Occupation

But to destroy the flowers is to destroy the lives of poor farmers. If wide and aggressive, such an assault could lead to a new jihad. Some observers have even credited the quick fall of the Taliban to the former regime's unpopular ban on poppy cultivation, a policy that left them with very few allies once the US bombs began falling.

Further complicating any real war on drugs would be the international community's open alliance with Afghanistan's mujahedeen warlords, or *jangsalaran*, many of whom might turn on the occupation if their sub rosa economic activities are attacked. As one US soldier in Kandahar explained to the *English Independent*, "We start taking out drug guys, and they will start taking out our guys." The security chief in Nangarhar, Hazrat Ali, a US ally, is said to be heavily involved in the drug trade. And now American officials have started to threaten him. "One day, he will wake up and find out he's out of business," Col. David Lamm, chief of staff for US forces in Afghanistan, said of Hazrat Ali in a recent press interview. If Hazrat Ali is targeted, it's unlikely that he'll go quietly.

Back in Wardak the impending war on poppy is viewed by the Muslim farmers as hypocritical and cruel. Just before we take leave of Nazir and his cousins, he asks me: "Why does America allow people to sell alcohol but not heroin? What is the difference? At least in Islam both are *haram*."

Women Are Struggling to Achieve Equality in Afghanistan

By Sadiqa Basiri, in an interview with Karla Mantilla

The Taliban, which ruled Afghanistan from 1996 to 2001, was one of the most oppressive regimes in recent history. Under Taliban rule, women were not allowed to be seen in public unless they were completely veiled, and even then only if they were accompanied by a male family member. Women were forbidden to work outside the home, be treated by a male physician, or go to school. The Taliban severely punished and sometimes killed women who did not follow the rules. When the Taliban government fell in late 2001, many people assumed that women would be able to participate more fully in public life. However, even though Afghanistan's new constitution provides equal rights for women, the majority of Afghan women still suffer from severe discrimination.

In the following selection journalist Karla Mantilla interviews Sadiqa Basiri, an Afghan women's rights activist. Basiri lived in Pakistan when the Taliban was in power but is now living in Afghanistan. In the interview Basiri describes some of the problems Afghan women face, including domestic violence, a lack of access to information about their rights, and illiteracy. However, Basiri points out that Afghan women are working hard to create a better future and that they have received some much-needed help from the international community. Karla Mantilla is a reporter for Off Our Backs *magazine.*

[*K**arla Mantilla*]: Tell me about your work and what you do in Afghanistan and in Pakistan.

[*Sadiqa Basiri*]: When I was done with high school,

Karla Mantilla, "The Current State of Afghanistan: An Interview with Sadiqa Basiri of the Afghan Women's Network," *Off Our Backs*, vol. 34, July/August 2004. Copyright © 2004 by Off Our Backs, Inc. Reproduced by permission.

I went to university to study medicine. But after a month, the university was closed because the Taliban had an influential role in the government of Pakistan. Then I began working to design the website for the Afghan Women's Network (AWN). And then for one year I worked as media officer and assistant director and now I'm working as an advocacy manager for AWN.

Apart from my work with AWN, I work for an education project in the provinces of Afghanistan. I founded the first girls' school in the Wardak province and am planning to open two more schools in the Wardak and Jalalabad provinces.

KM: The AWN represents a lot of different Afghan women's groups?

SB: It is an umbrella organization for women's groups who are operating in Afghanistan and Pakistan.

KM: Who funds the AWN?

SB: We were first funded in Afghanistan by NOVIB—a group from the Netherlands. Now we are mostly funded by the German government—GTZ, the German Technical Corporation, and by HBF, also German-based.

KM: But no American groups?

SB: We are funded by UNIFEM [United Nations Development Fund for Women].

KM: UNIFEM? But that's not really American.

SB: Yes, but they get funding from USAID [United States Agency for International Development].

KM: It's interesting that the United States went into Afghanistan saying we were going to do all this stuff to rebuild Afghanistan and now it is the Germans and Dutch who are funding AWN.

SB: We are not mainly funded yet by the U.S. but we are looking forward to getting some funding for our projects that we are working on, like our report to CEDAW.

KM: Oh right CEDAW, the Convention on the Elimination of All Forms of Discrimination Against Women, the one that the U.S. hasn't ratified.

SB: Yes, but we have signed it! And ratified it. Afghanistan signed CEDAW on March 5, 2003. So now our government is taking the lead on writing a report to the CEDAW committee, and the AWN is writing a shadow report that will go parallel to the government report.

KM: What interests do you see the U.S. as having in Afghanistan?

SB: In my opinion, the reason the U.S. has been interested in Afghanistan is because of the uranium we have. We have a lot of uranium in Afghanistan. In southern Afghanistan, there are airports which have been made for ISAF and the American armies where Afghan nationals are not allowed. But we get reports from the local people over there that soil is being taken, by plane, from Afghanistan.

KM: Soil rich in uranium?

SB: Yes, it is then being filtered. A kilo of uranium in our country can provide electricity for all of Kabul for a month. This could be the interest of the United States in Afghanistan and Iraq—a source of energy—it is clear to everyone that that's the plan.

Only a Few Women Have Real Opportunities

KM: What are the biggest problems that women are facing in Afghanistan right now?

SB: Safety, still. Women still can't travel 20 km away from home by themselves.

KM: Do you think most women in Afghanistan feel that things are better or worse now for women?

SB: Well, there is a huge change in the big cities. There are a lot of chances for women to work, to show their ability and to use their skills. But that is only for a few women, for women who had the possibility of education while under Taliban regime. Like my family, and myself—I lived during the Taliban government, but we were in Pakistan so I was able to go to school.

But for my cousins who live in a village in Afghanistan, there hasn't been any change in their lives during these last three years [since 2001].

KM: How do you think most women in Afghanistan—at least the women you have talked to—feel about the U.S. intervention, the U.S. bombing and getting rid of the Taliban?

SB: Well, I would say that for those women living in big cities or working with nonprofits they would feel, "Well, we lost our people during U.S. bombing, we had such a terrible year. We were bombed for nothing. We were not the attackers in New York and we are not terrorists, but we were bombed. We lost something, but then we found something. We got something now." Because the women in the cities know what is happening

in the country at large. The constitution has been written and
there are chances for women to work and there are chances for
women to raise their voice and ask for their rights.

But for women in the small cities, towns or in the provinces,
there is such a lack of information. There is no media that they
can use to be informed. There isn't any radio, there isn't any TV,
there aren't any newspapers, and anyway, most women are illiter-
ate. They are very far from what is happening so they are not
happy about the U.S. because they knew what happened in one
village during the U.S. bombing, that there was a wedding that
was bombed where hundreds of people were killed—children,
women, boys, girls, everyone.

KM: So how do you feel about the new government in Afghanistan now?

SB: We are thankful to President Karzai because he was the
person who could convince people to be with him in the transition in government. And our constitution has been written and
there are many good articles in it about women's rights. Once
those rights are implemented, we will have a very good country.

Afghanistan's Constitution

KM: Can you tell me a little bit about what the women's rights
provisions are?

SB: We have equal opportunities for men and women and 25
percent of the seats will be for women.

KM: That's better than here!

SB: Yes, it is a very rich constitution. It provides for two women
lawyers to represent each of our 34 provinces. It provides for com-
pulsory education for girls and boys, which is wonderful. Also, the
country is under the Islamic tradition, under Islamic rule, because
our people want their religion and they respect their religion.

Now that CEDAW has been signed and ratified, it will give a
lot of chances for women to work confidently and safely. We had
a very good constitution in 1964 but there were problems in implementation. For example, we had the family court but women
were not able to file their cases. So that constitution never came
into practice. If this constitution is not implemented, I'm very
afraid it would be like a wonderful book that would be put on
the shelf.

KM: Will there be a Sharia [fundamentalist Islamic law] court
system?

SB: Because our constitution is obeying Islamic law, there will be.

The Problem of Domestic Violence

KM: Do you have much domestic violence?

SB: A lot. It is very common—it is very, very common. It is so common that people really do not understand that it is domestic violence—they think that it is part of life. Last year in one of our refugee camps in Pakistan, a woman burned herself because of the problems she had in her home. She just poured oil on herself and burned herself.

KM: She was trying to commit suicide?

SB: Yes, the reason was the domestic violence in her house.

KM: So women don't have a sense that they should not be beaten?

SB: Right. It's terrible. Because there is no solution. Or, there would be a solution, but it would be very difficult. When a girl gets married she must stay in her husband's house until she dies. A married woman who comes back to her father's home is never respected in the neighborhood. People say that she was a bad wife, that she could not live with her husband and that she did not think of her children. And even her children are looked down upon.

KM: Wouldn't those people think that it was the child's father who did something bad?

SB: No. The understanding of people is such that they never blame the husband, unless something very specific is revealed.

KM: Are there shelters for battered women?

SB: No, we don't have shelters yet.

KM: How about for women who have been abducted or raped? What happens to them?

SB: It is so bad. They stay in jail, in prisons.

KM: The women who are raped? Why?

SB: Because, once it is known that a woman was raped, she will try to commit suicide. Or, she may be murdered.

KM: By whom?

SB: By her family or by the rapist. But most of the time it is not revealed when a woman is raped. But if it is, then the only place for her to go is in jail. A woman must stay in prison until someone thinks that it is okay to let her come out. Or her family makes a commitment that they will take care of her.

KM: So she is in jail for her protection?
SB: Yes, for her protection. Not for punishment.

ENDANGERED WOMEN AND CHILDREN

*In addition to facing starvation and natural disasters, women
and children have suffered violence and abuse at the hands of
Afghanistan's men during the country's turbulent recent past,
and that danger persists. The following excerpt from a 2003
Human Rights Watch report describes some of the horrors
Afghan women and children face.*

Sexual violence against women, girls, and boys [in Af-
ghanistan] is both frequent and almost never reported.
Women, girls, and boys are abducted outside of their
homes in broad daylight and sexually assaulted. In some
areas girls have been abducted on the way to school.
Women and girls are raped in their homes, typically during the evening or night during armed robberies. One
attack was seemingly intended to silence a women's
rights activist. . . .

   In Laghman province in March 2003 army troops
under Ismatullah, the commander of a military base in
Laghman, broke into the homes of two different
women, and apparently raped one of them. A woman
who talked extensively with the women afterwards said:
I asked her questions about what they did, and she cried
and said, "When a woman's hands and feet are tied, what
can she do? If I tell you what happened, what can you
do?" Two times I asked, and she said, "I want to keep it
to myself." Her wrists were black from being tied with
ropes. She told me, "I am afraid. Please don't say anything to the governor. I know each and every one of
them, and I am afraid they will kill me."

Human Rights Watch, "'Killing You Is a Very Easy Thing for Us': Human Rights Abuses in Southeast Afghanistan," July 29, 2003. www.hrw.
org/reports/2003/afghanistan0703.

KM: So she doesn't have to be in jail.

SB: Right, but that is the only place where she can stay protected.

KM: So the jail is kind of like a shelter.

SB: Right. But now the German government started building a shelter. And, also the European Union. They have plans.

Women Are Pressured to Marry

KM: Are there women there who don't get married?

SB: Almost every woman gets married.

KM: So are there women who just want to have a different life and not get married?

SB: Oh no, no. If a woman says, no, I'm not going to get married, her father or brother will not allow it. In our country it is our tradition as soon as you are an adult.

KM: What can American women do for Afghan women?

SB: They can do everything almost, because American women are very powerful. They are liberated; when they try to do things, they do their best to make sure that the thing actually happens. I see, in the media here, that women have a lot of influential roles in their country, practically.

But under the U.S. Constitution, women have less power. So, women in Afghanistan have a lot of power under our constitution, but that is only on paper—we don't have any power in reality. But women here have a lot more power in reality, although less on paper. If women in the United States had the power that has been given to the women in Afghanistan, I think there would be peace all over the world. Then they could do everything almost for the welfare of the whole globe. That is my belief. Because women are more honest. In the countries where there are more women [in power], there is less corruption. That is known. We women do not need to say that; people observe that. It is very difficult for men to work with women, because women will side against the corruption. So women have always been given less opportunity to work on the decision making level in the developing countries.

KM: How do Afghan women feel about American women?

SB: We really appreciate them. The kind of attention they have for Afghan women, for the whole of Afghanistan is highly, highly appreciated. We have seen women come from the United States to work in Afghanistan with nonprofits, especially with the local NGOs [nongovernmental organizations]. As volunteers and as advisors, they have done a wonderful job and we really appreciate that. The little attention that has in fact been given to women in Afghanistan is all due to the hard work of women in the U.S. That is our belief.

Prostitution

KM: How are the foreign military of other countries treating the Afghan women? Are there problems with all the military from other countries?

SB: It is always very common in the countries where the armies go from one place to another for prostitution to happen there. So, yes, it happens in Afghanistan. And we are very, very sad about that. Poor women who have lost their husbands, who have lost their sons, and are the only ones who bring the income to their house can resort to prostitution.

KM: Do Afghan men visit prostitutes? Or is it mostly a foreign thing?

SB: Mostly foreign. Some Afghan, but mostly foreign. Because who would provide access to the women? Prostitutes have to be contacted through an Afghan man, because they cannot be contacted directly. So of course there is a man who might be an Afghan national who facilitates this. We don't want Afghan women to be used as prostitutes, to be taken advantage of because of their poverty.

AIDS it is not common in Afghanistan, and we are very afraid of it. Until recently, we did not have HIV/AIDS in Afghanistan, but on June 10th [2004], we have on record that three people died of AIDS.

KM: How did they get it?

SB: A father gave it to two of his children.

Afghan Women Dream of a Better Life

KM: Do you have anything else you would like to say?

SB: The first is that the projects or strategic plans about the reconstruction of Afghanistan should not be made overseas. They should not be made in the United States. They should not be made in Germany, in Holland or in France. They should be made on the ground and they should be discussed with the indigenous people so that they are productive.

Second, Afghan women are working very hard. There is hope in their dreams. They are dreaming of a better life, a better future for their children and an educated Afghan nation. They shouldn't be ignored. Yet we see that the United States is ignoring Afghanistan, and everyone notices that in Afghanistan. We know that when the interests of the U.S. are finished, we will be completely forgotten again. And we will be in the worst situation which will never be cured or recovered from.

The Poverty of Afghan Children

BY SCOTT CARRIER

In addition to decades of war, Afghanistan has suffered two major earth-quakes, drought, and major flooding in the past several years. Tillable soil, businesses, homes, and roads were all damaged or destroyed. As a result of such man-made and natural calamities, a majority of the more than 22 million Afghanistan inhabitants live in poverty. Aid organizations such as Doctors Without Borders, the Red Cross, and Mercy Corps have worked diligently to bring food, water, and health care to the people, but the needs have exceeded the supplies. In addition, the murders of aid workers in the early 2000s have caused these organizations to withdraw many of their workers. In the following article journalist Scott Carrier describes the harsh conditions in which many of Afghanistan's children are living. Carrier is a contributor to National Public Radio. He has also written for Esquire *and* Rolling Stone *magazines.*

In Afghanistan there are young boys out in the desert far from any village, filling potholes in the highway. There's snow on the ground and the wind is blowing and the boys have rags for clothes and plastic slippers for shoes, and their shovels are made from mortar shells pounded out and lashed to a stick. There's a lot of freezing and thawing in Afghanistan in early winter, so the highway is periodically broken up into craters and ditches, and the traffic—trucks and taxis and Toyota Tacoma pickups with Northern Alliance [the militia alliance of northern Afghanistan] soldiers in the back—has to slow down and swerve snakelike through the obstacles. The boys are essentially working for the drivers, trying to make their trip faster and safer. When a vehicle approaches they stand in a hitchhike position waving one arm and one leg in semaphore fashion, and the drivers speed by at 60 or 90 miles an hour cracking their windows and pushing money into the wind—old, dirty afghanis worth 2 cents—and the boys race to see who can get to the money first. It's a good job, compared to others.

I remember a boy, maybe seven years old, by the blue mosque in Mazar-i-Sharif last November [2001] whose pants and coat were caked with grease, his face and hands were black and his hair was like a used Brillo pad. The sun was going down, the evening prayer had just finished, the day's fast (as it was Ramadan) was over, and maybe the kid was on his way home for dinner, if there was any dinner. Of course, he hit me up for some money, holding out his hand but too tired to fake or show any emotion. All I had were $20 bills, and so I told him no. He shadowed me for a while, trying to come up with an idea, his stomach telling his mind to think, to do something. If I gave him a twenty I'd never make it back to the hotel. I would have been surrounded by hands and eyes, pleading, shouting, pressing closer and closer. It was hard to look at the boy, and I wondered how he got so filthy. But now, . . . I realize he may have been repacking the wheel bearings or putting new brakes on a large truck.

Children Struggle to Survive

In Afghanistan, the average life expectancy is 46 years, or about 30 years less than in the United States. The birth rate is 5.8 children per woman. The average yearly income per capita is $280. The country is landlocked, separated from areas of commerce by huge mountain ranges and endless deserts, and it has just emerged from a severe, three-year drought that in some areas killed half the crops and up to 80 percent of the livestock. In better years, Afghanistan exported fruits and nuts, cotton, and semiprecious gems, but now its only exports are opium and heroin, and in these it is a world leader. The middle and upper classes of its society fled the country years ago, and the remaining masses are heavily armed. They still have no new constitution, no system of laws, no real government.

Approximately 90 percent of children in Afghanistan do not go to school. After 23 years of war, the adult male population has been decimated, and the Taliban regime, in control of the country for nearly six years, banned all women from the workforce, so many kids have taken the place of their fathers and mothers as breadwinners for their families. In 1995 there were 28,000 children working on the streets of Kabul. By 1999 there were 50,000, and the number is thought to be much higher now. Some hammer sheet metal, some shine shoes or beg or collect scrap metal from the garbage in the street. Some build coffins. In rural areas they help by herding animals and by collecting paper and firewood. Some of these practices expose children to the danger of landmines. More than 1 out of every 4 children in Afghanistan will die before their fifth birthday; more than half are moderately or severely stunted from malnutrition. Something like 45 percent of both the Taliban and Northern Alliance armies were children under the age of 18. And a UNICEF [the United Nations Children's Fund] study has found that the majority of children are highly traumatized and expect to die before reaching adulthood.

So it comes as no surprise to learn that in Afghanistan children live like slaves. If you tell me that they work from sunup to sundown and make only 5 cents an hour performing dangerous tasks that eventually kill them, my first reaction is: I bet they are glad to get paid at all.

Kabul After the Taliban

By Jon Lee Anderson

The Soviet occupation of Kabul in the 1970s and 1980s, civil war, and the rule of the Taliban left the capital city in bad shape. In addition, the artillery and air bombardment and street fighting during the U.S. war on Afghanistan destroyed 75 percent of Kabul. The fall of the Taliban ended a tyrannical regime, but left the city's residents struggling to resume ordinary life. In this excerpt from his book The Lion's Grave: Dispatches from Afghanistan, *Jon Lee Anderson describes visiting Kabul as its citizens worked to rebuild the city after the Taliban had been defeated. He notes that although some of the people he met freely criticized the old government, others were still fearful that they would be attacked if they discussed the oppression of the Taliban. Anderson also discusses his conversation with Salahuddin Rabbani, the son of former Afghan president Burhanuddin Rabbani. Salahuddin states that he is hopeful that Afghanistan will be able to forge a new democratic government. Jon Lee Anderson, a freelance writer for the* New Yorker *magazine, is the author of* The Fall of Baghdad.

The tomb of Ahmed Shah Massoud is in a shallow cave burrowed into a hill in the Panjshir Valley. The grave site, which is near the edge of a crude road cut along the steep valley slopes, is marked by a green sign with hand lettering that spells out "Chief of the Martyr's Hill" in Farsi and in English. The Panjshir Valley—a canyon some hundred and twenty miles long, stretching southwest from northern Afghanistan to the Shamali plain, just north of Kabul—is a bleakly rugged place. The road often falls away or is narrowed by mud slides, and ruined Soviet-era military tanks and armored personnel carriers litter the route, along with the twisted carcasses of trucks and jeeps that have slipped off the road onto the rocks below.

Jon Lee Anderson, *The Lion's Grave: Dispatches from Afghanistan.* New York: Grove Press, 2002. Copyright © 2002 by Jon Lee Anderson. All rights reserved. Reproduced by permission.

Massoud was born in Bazarak, a village less than a mile up the Panjshir River from Martyr's Hill. He was a national hero long before he was murdered, on September 9th [2001], and he has since become a figure of quasi-religious dimensions. Travelling down the valley toward Kabul at the beginning of December with several other journalists, I noticed that my driver, Enam, who is a native Panjshiri, had tied a black flag of mourning to the antenna of our jeep. There was a Massoud poster plastered to the windshield, practically obscuring it, and a small photograph of Massoud taped onto the driver's-side window. We were part of a convoy of seventeen vehicles, many of which were decorated in a similar fashion.

It had taken us four days to travel about two hundred and fifty miles—south from the city of Taloqan, over the Hindu Kush, and into the Panjshir Valley—across an isolated, edgy region where the Northern Alliance seemed to have only a tenuous presence. On the fourth day, the sun was setting on Massoud's grave as we made our way toward the paved road that crosses the plain to Kabul. Once we were on the road, our headlights illuminated blasted vehicles, ruined tanks, collapsed houses, and broken walls covered with starbursts from shell fire and pocked by bullets. After the Taliban took Kabul, in 1996, they destroyed all the villages in the Shamali, emptying the area of civilians and creating a buffer zone for their front line with the Northern Alliance, which forayed out from the Panjshir. In the weeks leading up to the Taliban's retreat from Kabul, in mid-November, the frontline positions had been heavily pounded by American bombers and warplanes, and the road was gouged and cratered. Enam drove slowly and weaved around the holes, but was careful not to get too close to the edge of the road. Newly posted signs warned of land mines.

Kabul appeared out of the night, shockingly, as we reached the top of a small cluster of hills that rose from the plain. There was light everywhere. Glowing squares and rectangles of white, blue, and yellow crossed the valley. It was the first Afghan city I had seen with a functioning electrical system.

Postwar Kabul

With the Taliban gone, Kabul has reverted to being the one city in Afghanistan where, in relative terms, almost anything goes. Liquor is still forbidden and scarce, but it's available. Street vendors sell postcards of sultry Indian screen idols, and cockfights have resumed. Metalworkers are doing a brisk business in satellite dishes, which are hand-beaten from scrap; the finished products are covered with the logos and brand names of canned goods, making them look like pop art. The cult of Massoud is also flourishing. Throngs of young men scuffled for tickets to the premiere of a French documentary, *Massoud l'Afghan*, and an official morning of homage was held recently at several of Kabul's main mosques. Northern Alliance soldiers laden with Massoud posters tucked them under the windshield wipers of cars, like parking tickets.

Yet there seems to be an underlying uncertainty about the changes that have taken place so suddenly. A British reporter and I were walking around downtown one morning, and we stopped on a street where there were several washing-machine and appliance-repair shops. My companion decided to interview a twelve-year-old boy who was working as a repairman. A group of curious men and boys soon surrounded us, and I noticed that four women in blue burkhas had paused to watch as well, from a short distance away. After a few minutes, the women came forward, and one of them, who said her name was Shahkoko and that she was forty-five years old, asked if we knew of any foreign aid agencies or NGOs [nongovernmental organizations] that needed English-speaking Afghan personnel. She had once been a teacher, she said, and under the Taliban had continued teaching, clandestinely, in her home, to help her family survive. But she had been discovered, and the Taliban had detained her teenage son, beaten him, and cut him with knives. So she had stopped giving her illegal classes. Now she was desperate to find real, paying work again. I took down her name, and two men who were listening helped me sort out some confusion over her street address.

Suddenly, we were interrupted by an irascible bearded man who owned one of the shops. He yelled at Yama, my translator, who is from northern Afghanistan. The bearded man was a Pashtun—a member of the tribal group that most of the Taliban are also from—and he excoriated Yama for helping foreigners talk to Afghan women. Yama was a yokel from Badakhshan Province, he said, which was an insulting reference to Yama's Tajik heritage. This upset Yama, who tried to pull me away, but by then I was angry, and I cursed the man and called him a "Talib." Shahkoko, the former teacher, nodded her head vigorously. "Thank you," she whispered. "You are right, he is a Talib." Then she and her friends moved quickly down the street, away from us and the little mob scene. My companions and I went in the opposite direction, leaving the shopkeeper blustering on the pavement. Yama chastised me for my outburst. "You cannot talk this way in Kabul yet," he said. "It is not safe for you. There are still many people here who think like the Taliban do."

Westerners Come Back to Kabul

It must be strange for many of the citizens of Kabul to be dealing with Western expectations when until only a few weeks ago the only foreigners in the city—or in the country, for that matter—were the Pakistanis, Chechens, Uzbeks, and Arabs fighting alongside the Taliban and [terrorist leader] Osama bin Laden's Al Qaeda organization. They have all vanished, and in their place are several hundred journalists from all over the world, who have packed the city's few hotels, rented scores of cars, and hired numerous translators. On the curb outside the Herat Restaurant, a kebab-and-pilaf place whose walls are adorned with old black-and-white photographs of Afghanistan's principal ancient sites (except for the destroyed Bamian Buddhas, which are curiously absent, as if they had never existed), a contingent of beggar boys and women in dirty burkhas are on permanent stakeout. The Herat is said to have been the favorite dining spot of the foreign Taliban in the capital, before the journalists came.

In the residential district of Wazir Akbar Khan, where carefully laid out tree-lined streets and public parks recall a time when Kabul was almost a modern city, workmen are busy repainting and restoring dilapidated houses for media organizations. There is a *Newsweek* house, a *New York Times* house, and an ABC and CBS house. A British journalist who is setting up a Kabul office for his television news agency has rented a house in which one of Osama bin Laden's wives used to live. The United Nations has resumed its operations, as have a number of international relief agencies, and foreign embassies are reopening. The Russians, British, Iranians, Turks, French, and Germans were among the first to come back, and in mid-December a group of American marines went into the U.S. embassy compound, which had been closed since 1989. The marines swept the grounds for unexploded ordnance and set up machine-gun nests behind sandbags on the roof.

A single concrete office tower rises some eighteen stories above the city center. It is the Telecommunications Ministry, Kabul's tallest building, and perhaps the last vestige of the days when Afghanistan seemed to have some kind of future. Architecturally, it is as though time had stopped in Kabul in the late seventies. Nothing much appears to have been constructed since then, except for dingy Soviet-built apartment blocks, and one half-finished bank building and a mosque, both begun under the Taliban.

The Wasteland of War

A great deal has been destroyed. One day while I was driving around the city with Fridoun, an affable twenty-three-year-old medical student, I remarked that he was born just about the time that the war against the Communists began—the jihad that was followed by civil war. "Yes," he said. "All I know is war. For me, rockets and bombings—all these things are normal." He shrugged. He was eager for Kabul's medical school to reopen, so that he could finish his studies and become a doctor. As we drove along the Kabul River, which has for several years been nearly bone-dry because of a drought, and began to circle the city, the scale of the destruction was overwhelming. Entire sections of Kabul have been obliterated. Block after block of buildings is a dismal ruin of bricks and twisted concrete; roofs have caved in, façades are full of bullet holes or have been pierced by tank shells. Fridoun explained what had caused each piece of devastation, and after a while it seemed as though we were examining the city the way one assesses the age of a dead tree by counting the rings in its stump.

Fridoun pointed out the beat-up tomb of King Nadir Shah—the father of Zahir Shah, who is now in exile in Rome—on a large dirt hill not far away. The hill was honeycombed with abandoned dugouts and fortifications, and sparsely adorned with martyrs' flags. It had been one of the front lines in the fighting over Kabul that began in 1992, when President Burhanuddin Rabbani and [Ahmed Shah] Massoud took power. The ruined buildings, lone walls, and solitary columns below the hill resembled giant sand castles or sections of an archaeological dig. "This area used to be very famous as a place of business for people coming in from the provinces," Fridoun said. "There were many hotels and shops." Now several ragged men and children were selling scrap metal and recycled spare parts for cars; bicycle repairmen sat on boxes at the roadside next to inner tubes, waiting for customers.

Fridoun said that Gulbuddin Hekmatyar, a Pashtun Muslim fundamentalist backed by Pakistan and Saudi Arabia (and, during the anti-Soviet jihad in the nineteen-eighties, by the CIA), had established a base in the mountains fringing the city beyond the hill, and from there he was able to rain rockets on the population, which he did with vicious abandon—even though he was officially the prime minister of the mujahideen government during this period. Massoud was at first assisted in the defense of the city by the Uzbek warlord Abdul Rashid Dostum, who had fought with the Soviets against the mujahideen until 1992, when he switched sides, thereby facilitating Massoud's seizure of Kabul. Dostum switched sides again in 1994. From the same hill where he had fought with Massoud against Hekmatyar, Dostum now turned his guns against Massoud. Then the Taliban attacked Hekmatyar and Dostum from behind. They retreated, and Massoud faced the Taliban and another mujahideen faction, the Hazara— ethnic Shias—who were entrenched in western Kabul, around the university. "What people say," Fridoun explained, "is that Massoud told the Taliban, 'Let's join together and finish the Hazara.'" In any case, he said, the Taliban began fighting with the Hazara, killed their leader, and Massoud chased them out of the city. "Then," Fridoun continued, "Massoud attacked the Taliban."

Fridoun went on in this manner as we drove into the devastated western suburbs, and I stopped trying to keep track of the precise chronology of what destruction was caused when and by whom. The result, in the end, was the same. All of the devastation had a name attached to it, and most of the names were still key figures in Afghanistan's politics. As we passed the former Soviet Cultural Center, Fridoun pointed across the road to a large building that had been peppered by gunfire. "This was where the Hazara killed their prisoners when they were in control here. They killed them by shooting, by *halal*, as we say"—Fridoun drew an imaginary knife across his throat—"by fire, by boiling water, and even by driving nails into heads."

I asked Fridoun how he felt about showing me the ruins. "I feel ashamed," he replied. "I feel ashamed that a foreign person sees this and thinks: This was destroyed by Afghans themselves." Then what did he think about the men who had done this, men who were still wielding power? "We know this is their last chance to be here with guns," he said softly. "If there are elections in Afghanistan for a new government, none of these people will be voted for. The people are very angry with these men. Right now, I know, if I say 'Massoud is bad' in Kabul, I will go to prison. But if democracy comes I can say who is bad and who is good, and I can vote for whoever I want to lead Afghanistan. . . .

Meeting at the Presidential Palace

The Afghan presidential palace is in the sprawling, parklike nineteenth-century royal compound in downtown Kabul. The grounds of the complex are unkempt now, and the roofs of several buildings have caved in, apparently because they were hit by rockets, or perhaps tank fire. I went there to speak to President Rabbani's eldest son, Salahuddin, whom I had met several weeks earlier in Faizabad. He had accompanied his father to Kabul when the Taliban left. I waited for Salahuddin in a room that had a huge gray metal Soviet-era intercom system clumsily inscribed with Cyrillic lettering. It clashed with the crystal chandelier, heavy curtains, Persian carpets, and gilded furniture. Salahuddin greeted me in the private presidential meeting room. It was the first time, he said, he had talked to someone there, and he seemed to be enjoying himself. The room was dark and cold, but there was a small, Russian-made electric heater in the corner that made it bearable.

Salahuddin said that he had not been back to London since September, and that he hoped his family would join him in Afghanistan, perhaps next summer. He was diplomatic about the new government and about his father's position. "I'd say that my father is not angry," he said, "but that he is not entirely happy, either." They approved of [President] Hamid Karzai as the new leader, but would have liked what Salahuddin described as broader representation for other members of the Northern Alliance. He shrugged and smiled. "I think there was pressure for a quick fix in Afghanistan, and you know that no such thing is possible here."

I asked Salahuddin what he thought was going to happen. "All I can tell you is that my father is ready to hand over power," he said. "But as for the rest I cannot say." A Northern Alliance security official who had been close to Massoud had told me privately that the day after the Bonn agreement was announced, General Fahim became so angry about Rabbani's complaints that he threatened to arrest him. Fahim backed down, but he told Rabbani to stay in his residence and to shut up. Fahim had also issued some kind of ultimatum to General Dostum, and, coincidentally or not, several days later Dostum told reporters that he had no intention of spilling blood over his differences with the new government.

Salahuddin said he had hoped that the UN would not attempt to impose a disarmament process, and in fact that possibility had been left out of the final text of the Bonn agreement. "What do you think," Salahuddin said, "that the Blue Helmets [UN soldiers] would be able to come and say to the people, 'Give me your gun'? The gun is more than about power and survival; to Afghans having a gun is a source of pride. You can't just take them away. So this is impossible in Afghanistan." He had also been troubled by the preliminary language for one of the clauses of the agreement, which he described as calling for justice against perpetrators of past atrocities. "This is a real problem," be said. "How to define atrocities. There are many commanders who have killed people who might fear that they could now be considered war criminals. Our soldiers have killed a lot of Taliban. Does that constitute an atrocity?" This argument prevailed in Bonn, and the final version of the pact didn't address retribution.

After we had chatted awhile, Salahuddin said, rather abruptly, "Now I have a question for you. What is your opinion of my prospects for a political future here in Afghanistan?" In Faizabad, people had referred to Salahuddin—although not in his presence—as "the Vice President," and I had once told him so. He had laughed then, and looked pleased. Now it was less of a joke.

I told Salahuddin that I thought that Afghanistan's older generation of political leaders had failed abysmally, and that his country needed the ideas of a new generation of people who were educated and knowledgeable about the modern world but were also in touch with their own culture.

"That is what I have been thinking, too," Salahuddin said.

As he was showing me out, Salahuddin introduced me to the palace's oldest employee, a bearded man in his late sixties who wore a coat with shiny buttons and who stood at attention as we passed. He had been at the palace since the time of King Zahir Shah, Salahuddin said, although he had been dismissed by the Taliban. The Rabbanis had asked him to return. He and Salahuddin bantered about presidential secrets, and Salahuddin described one of the important events that the old retainer had witnessed: the moment in 1959 when Queen Homaira, King Zahir Shah's wife and the leader of a movement to liberate modern Afghan women, threw off her veil. The old man nodded, confirming this, but kept silent.

CHRONOLOGY

3000 B.C.
Bronze Age civilization flourishes in Mundigak, near what is now Kandahar, and in Deh Morasi Ghundai.

2000 B.C.
A city is founded on the site of Kabul. Iron goods and weapons are manufactured in Afghanistan.

522 B.C.
The Persian Achaemenid ruler Darius the Great invades and conquers Afghanistan.

329 B.C.
The Macedonian general Alexander the Great arrives, overthrowing several satraps of the Achaemenid Empire of Persia.

327 B.C.
Alexander the Great retreats to the Indus Valley in what is now Pakistan. A Greek state survives in Bactria, northern Afghanistan.

135 B.C.
The Kushans begin their conquest of Bactria. Under Kanishka, a Kushan leader, the Buddhist religion arrives in Afghanistan several centuries after its founding in northern India.

A.D. 400
An invasion of central Asian nomads, the White Huns, sweeps through Afghanistan, overthrowing the Kushan rulers.

652
The first Arab Muslims arrive in Afghanistan. Islam is established, replacing the Buddhist culture that was weakened by the White Hun invasion.

962
The Ghaznavid dynasty in Afghanistan, is established.

1186
The Ghaznavid dynasty falls to an invasion led by Alaudin of
  Ghur. The Ghurid dynasty begins its reign in Afghanistan.

1219
The Mongol Genghis Khan leads his armies through central Asia
  and Afghanistan, leveling the leading cities of the Ghurid dynasty and putting entire city populations to death.

1332
The Ghurid rulers return to Afghanistan after the Mongol
  Ilkhanate of Persia weakens.

1504
Afghanistan is conquered by the Mogul ruler Babur, whose state
  covers what is now Pakistan and northern India.

1622
The Safavid dynasty of Persia controls western Afghanistan. A
  revolt of the Afghan tribes against Mogul rule simmers in
  the rest of the country through the seventeenth century.

1747
After many years of revolt against Safavid rule, the Durrani Empire, the first cohesive Afghan state, is established, with Ahmad Shah as Afghanistan's first Pashtun ruler. During his
  reign Ahmad Shah Durrani defeats the Moguls in eastern Afghanistan and creates the largest state in central Asia.

1836
The British invade Afghanistan and in 1839 install a puppet king,
  Shah Shoja, as the ruler of Afghanistan. The king will be
  killed three years later during the First Anglo-Afghan War.

1838–1842
Great Britain and Afghanistan engage in the First Anglo-Afghan
  War.

1878–1880
In the Second Anglo-Afghan War, the British capture Kabul and
  by the Treaty of Gandamak are allowed a representative in

Kabul. Soon after the resident is murdered, the British with-draw from Afghanistan.

1919

Emir Habibullah Khan is murdered at the instigation of the British. Under his successor, Emir Amanullah Khan, Afghan-istan declares its independence from Great Britain, sparking the Third Anglo-Afghan War.

1921

The British retreat from Afghanistan.

1928

Religious leaders under the leadership of Habibullah Kalakani revolt against Amanullah, who abdicates and flees the coun-try. Kalakani is murdered by Nadir Khan, who establishes control of the country.

1933

Nadir Khan is assassinated, and his son Zahir Shah is declared the new king of Afghanistan.

1965

A new constitution is adopted and the first nationwide elections are held.

1973

Zahir Shah is overthrown by his brother-in-law and former prime minister Muhammad Daud, who declares the found-ing of a republic.

1978

Communist opponents in the People's Democratic Party of Af-ghanistan assassinate Daud and overthrow his government.

1979

The Soviet Union invades Afghanistan to secure its Communist regime against revolt on the part of Muslim leaders and mu-jahideen, or holy warriors. The Soviets establish military bases, take control of Kabul, and begin fighting a guerrilla war in the countryside.

1989

The Soviet army withdraws from Afghanistan. Mujahideen groups form a patchwork of independent fiefs in the countryside, although the Soviet-backed regime in Kabul survives.

1992

Mujahideen groups take control of Kabul and declare the founding of an Islamic state under the presidency of Burhanuddin Rabbani.

1996

A group of exiled Islamic students and mullahs known as the Taliban seizes control of Kabul. A strict fundamentalist regime is established, decreeing sharia, or Islamic judicial precepts as interpreted by the mullahs, to be the new law of the land. A small pocket of resistance known as the Northern Alliance remains in control of key roads and checkpoints in northern Afghanistan. The Taliban gives shelter to Osama bin Laden, a Saudi and founder of the terrorist organization al Qaeda, after Bin Laden flees the Sudan.

2001

Despite international protest, the Taliban destroys two historic Buddha statues in the Bamian valley. In September opposition leader Ahmed Shah Massoud is assassinated. On September 11 al Qaeda terrorists mount a devastating terrorist attack on the United States. The United States demands that the Taliban hand over Osama bin Laden, but this demand is refused. In October the Northern Alliance and a U.S.-led coalition attack government and military targets in Afghanistan. In November the Northern Alliance marches on Kabul and overthrows the regime. Under the Bonn Agreement, an Afghan Interim Authority is established, and in December the Pashtun leader Hamid Karzai is declared head of the interim government.

2002

A *loya jirga*, or council, of tribal leaders and government ministers begins hammering out a new Afghan constitution.

2003

The new Afghan constitution is adopted in December 2003.

2004

On January 4 the *loya jirga* agrees on the new constitution, creating a strong presidency and giving the parliament the power to appoint cabinet ministers. The presidential election takes place on October 9 and proceeds largely without disruption, although several opponents of Karzai declare the vote a fraud. On November 3 Karzai is declared the official winner of the presidential election. On December 7 Karzai is sworn in as the president of Afghanistan.

FOR FURTHER RESEARCH

Ancient and Medieval History

Ludwig Adamec, *Historical Dictionary of Afghanistan.* Lanham, MD: Scarecrow, 1997.

Clifford Edmund Bosworth, *The Later Ghaznavids: Splendor and Decay: The Dynasty in Afghanistan and Northern India, 1040–1186.* New York: Columbia University Press, 1977.

Martin Ewans, *Afghanistan: A Short History of Its People and Politics.* New York: HarperCollins, 2002.

Arnold Fletcher, *Afghanistan: Highway of Conquest.* Ithaca, NY: Cornell University Press, 1965.

Stephen Tanner, *Afghanistan: A Military History from Alexander the Great to the Taliban.* New York: Perseus, 2003.

Colonial Period

Vartan Gregorian, *The Emergence of Modern Afghanistan: Politics of Reform and Modernization, 1880–1946.* Stanford, CA: Stanford University Press, 1969.

William Habberton, *Anglo-Russian Relations Concerning Afghanistan, 1837–1907.* Urbana: University of Illinois Press, 1937.

Peter Hopkirk, *The Great Game: The Struggle for Empire in Central Asia.* New York: Kodansha International, 1992.

Rhea Talley Stewart, *Fire in Afghanistan, 1914–1929: Faith, Hope, and the British Empire.* Garden City, NY: Doubleday, 1973.

Twentieth-Century History to the Soviet Invasion

Henry S. Bradsher, *Afghanistan and the Soviet Union.* Durham, NC: Duke University Press, 1983.

David B. Edwards, *Before Taliban: Genealogies of the Afghan Jihad.* Berkeley: University of California Press, 2002.

Sandy Gall, *Afghanistan: Agony of a Nation.* London: Bodley Head, 1988.

M. Hasan Kakar, *Afghanistan: The Soviet Invasion and the Afghan Response, 1979–1982.* Berkeley: University of California Press, 1995.

Jeri Laber, *"A Nation Is Dying": Afghanistan Under the Soviets, 1979–1987.* Evanston, IL: Northwestern University Press, 1988.

Oleg Sarin, *The Afghan Syndrome: The Soviet Union's Vietnam.* Novato, CA: Presidio, 1993.

Sirdar Ikbal Ali Shah, *Afghanistan of the Afghans.* London: Octagon, 1982.

The Taliban

Jon Lee Anderson, *The Lion's Grave: Dispatches from Afghanistan.* New York: Grove, 2002.

Steve Coll, *Ghost Wars: The Secret History of the CIA, Afghanistan, and bin Laden, from the Soviet Invasion to September 10, 2001.* New York: Penguin, 2004.

Larry P. Goodson, *Afghanistan's Endless War: State Failure, Regional Politics, and the Rise of the Taliban.* Seattle: University of Washington Press, 2001.

Robert D. Kaplan, *Soldiers of God: With the Mujahidin in Afghanistan.* Boston: Houghton Mifflin, 1990.

Kurt Lohbeck, *Holy War, Unholy Victory: Eyewitness to the CIA's Secret War in Afghanistan.* Washington, DC: Regnery Gateway, 1993.

William Maley, *The Afghanistan Wars.* New York: Palgrave Macmillan, 2002.

Roland and Sabrina Michaud. *Afghanistan: The Land That Was.* New York: Harry N. Abrams, 2002.

Angelo Rasanayagam. *Afghanistan: A Modern History.* London: I.B. Tauris, 2003.

Ahmed Rashid, *Taliban: Militant Islam, Oil, and Fundamentalism in Central Asia*. New Haven, CT: Yale University Press, 2000.

Amanda Roraback, *Afghanistan in a Nutshell*. Santa Monica, CA: Enisen, 2004.

After the Taliban

Chris Johnson and Jolyon Leslie. *Afghanistan: The Mirage of Peace*. New York: Zed Books, 2005.

Alexander Klaits and Gulchin Gulmamadova-Klaits, *Love and War in Afghanistan*. New York: Seven Stories, 2005.

Christina Lamb, *The Sewing Circles of Herat: A Personal Voyage Through Afghanistan*. New York: HarperCollins, 2002.

Chris Mackey and Greg Miller, *The Interrogators: Inside the Secret War Against al Qaeda*. New York: Little, Brown, 2004.

Robin Moore, *The Hunt for Bin Laden*. New York: Random House, 2003.

Anne M. Todd, *Major World Leaders: Hamid Karzai*. Philadelphia: Chelsea House, 2003.

Web Sites

Afgha.com, www.afgha.com. Large news and article archive, listed under subject headings such as Elections, Human Rights, and Military Situation, as well as message boards and a chat room for Afghan-related topics.

Afghanistan News.Net, http://afghanistannews.net. A digest of news stories and features dealing with Afghanistan, the Middle East, and Central Asia.

Afghanistan Online, www.afghan-web.com. General information on Afghanistan history, government and politics, economy, culture, and business, including a page of biographies and an Afghan Woman page.

Afghanistan's Web Site, www.afghanistans.com. General information about Afghanistan, including news, photographs, flags and stamps, a page of Afghan proverbs, music, and links to other Afghan-related Web sites.

Radio Afghanistan, www.radioafghanistan.com. Streaming radio broadcast with news in several languages and music.

Revolutionary Association of the Women of Afghanistan, www. rawa.org. An organization fighting for women's rights, democracy, and education in Afghanistan. The site describes current projects, publications, and events and allows visitors to browse through documents and writing related to women's issues.

INDEX